Inking the Deal

Inking the Deal

A Guide for Successful Academic Publishing

Stanley E. Porter

BAYLOR UNIVERSITY PRESS

© 2010 by Baylor University Press
Waco, Texas 76798-7363

Cover Design by Trudi Gershinov, TG Design
Cover image: Matthias Tunger/Photographer's Choice/Getty Images.
Book Design by Diane Smith

Library of Congress Cataloging-in-Publication Data

Porter, Stanley E., 1956-
 Inking the deal : a guide for successful academic publishing / Stanley E.
Porter.
     p. cm.
 Includes index.
 ISBN 978-1-60258-265-1 (pbk.)
 1. Scholarly publishing. 2. Scholarly publishing--United States.
3. Communication in learning and scholarship--Technological innova-
tions. I. Title.
 Z286.S37P67 2010
 070.5--dc22

                          2010000794

Printed in the United States of America on acid-free paper.

I wish to dedicate this book to
Professor David J. A. Clines,
who gave me a unique opportunity in publishing and
taught me so much about the business

TABLE OF CONTENTS

Foreword

I want to thank several people who helped to motivate me to write this book. One was David Williams, then a master's-level student and now a graduate of my academic institution. The other was Jamie Robertson, then a master's-level student and now a doctoral-level student at my institution. They knew that I was both an active publishing scholar and interested in helping others to become published authors as well, and they on different occasions asked and encouraged me to put on a seminar to help students interested in following this path. I was pleased that so many students attended the first seminar, and then others since. I had the opportunity to reflect on twenty years of writing and publishing experience, and to collect my thoughts together into a cohesive and coherent presentation. That seminar led to subsequent iterations of this seminar, as free-standing presentations and as part of courses on research methods for advanced research students wanting to become scholars. Each presentation led me to refine what I had originally said. A number of those who heard these presentations have taken its advice seriously and gone on to publish—the start of a publishing career. I have had the privilege of working together with many of these students, as they have taken up my offer of working collaboratively with them as they, too, have begun the process of becoming active, publishing scholars.

I also want to thank several people who have further promoted the writing of this manuscript. There were several people who, having heard me present the material that is now found in this book, encouraged me to write it down in a form that would be more accessible to others. These include especially my wife, Wendy, who remains my first and best proofreader.

I have dedicated this book to Professor David J. A. Clines. He gave me the opportunity to be employed as the senior academic editor at Sheffield Academic Press (SAP), and to learn the publishing business from the inside. David and those who conceived of SAP created and realized a great vision for academic publishing that now continues in Sheffield Phoenix Press. I have appreciated the opportunities to work with David in this common endeavor for the best part of nearly twenty years.

Lastly, I wish to thank my publisher, Dr. Carey Newman of Baylor University Press. When I approached him about this project, he was a little skeptical—not because of what I was saying, but because he had his own perspective on academic publishing. As we discussed our perspectives further, it became clear to me that we did not have perspectives that were at variance, but that were complementary—and, we think, necessary to get out into the wider field of academic consideration. I want to thank Carey for undertaking to publish this volume, and Baylor University Press for adding this volume to their list as they continue to expand their scope and increase their impact on academic publishing. I realize that some of the things that I say in what follows are hard on some publishers, including their editors. Those who have worked with Carey will know that he breaks these molds.

I use numerous stories and anecdotes throughout this book. Details have often been changed to make them less specific and more widely pertinent.

The source that has proved most helpful—often because it has reinforced my own perspective—is the *Chronicle of Higher Education*, whose articles I regularly access online. I have cited a number of its articles and could have cited a number of others. I encourage interested readers to check their Web site.

One feature that I am unable to include fully in this volume is my seminars or workshops on writing. Feel free to contact me at porters@ mcmaster.ca if you would like me to come to your area or institution to run a seminar or workshop that addresses or expands upon the topics discussed in this volume. There is much more to be said! I have developed writing seminars—two English degrees and several years of teaching college English have certainly not gone to waste—where I examine the current writing profiles of faculty, develop collaborative and critical workshop experiences, work with you individually to develop a publication plan, examine some of your past and current writing to help you as you continue to write for publication, make suggestions regarding the possible venues for your publications, and then work to develop collaborative and accountability publication plans. If you are interested in having me come to do one of these workshops at your institution, please do not hesitate to contact me. These seminars can extend from a half day on up, depending on the number of faculty or other interested individuals involved. I would welcome the opportunity to work with academics who want to improve their publishing profiles and initiate a publishing lifestyle.

One caveat—what I write in these pages is *not* a guaranteed formula for success in academic publishing. I have marshaled a number of ideas that I have learned in the course of my career. I make no guarantees or claims that they will all work out or that they will work for you. However, they have worked well for me, and I have seen them work well for others, and so I pass them on to you to use as you please.

Introduction

About This Book

This is a straightforward—even at times hard-hitting—book about successful academic publishing in journals and books. It is expressly designed and written for you who wish to become successful academic authors especially in the areas of biblical studies, theology and religion, and the arts and humanities. Academic publishing is at the heart of the advancement of learning in the intellectual world. Academic publishing provides the venue where the newest ideas are proposed and developed, and where scholars intellectually expose themselves to the scrutiny of their peers to see if their ideas can pass muster. There is a certain amount of ego strength required to lay out your ideas in print, and it can be daunting to the point of complete paralysis if you are not experienced at it or ready for it. This book is written with the intention of helping, first, those who have not yet developed an active publishing profile in the serious academic world to work toward such a publishing lifestyle and, secondly, those who have not yet achieved their potential to develop further their academic publishing life—all of this based on my own experience and what I have learned as an editor, author, and active academic. By learning how to do so, unnecessary impediments can be minimized, and scholars—including you—can put forward their best work for the benefit of the profession and their own individual research profiles.

Writing this book, which is focused primarily upon academic publishing, does not *necessarily* mean that I do not have respect for those who write for a popular audience (I do have an opinion, but that's another story). The criteria for publishing popular writing, however, have much more to do with finding subjects that are hot at the time, knowing the right people in the publishing business, timing the market, dumbing down the content of one's work, and then dumbing it down again. Most of all, whereas it may pay you well as an author, it makes little to no contribution to the advancement of knowledge and understanding of a subject. If you are interested in learning how to write for the popular book market, or the popular press, I suggest that you find an agent (who probably will only represent you if you are an established author—wait a minute, how does this work?—and will take 15–20 percent of the money from *your* writing), forget your most challenging and provocative ideas, develop a slick prose style, and cultivate your media image. If, instead, you are interested in how to begin to publish successfully in the academic market, and possibly even to establish a widespread, well-earned, and deserved reputation for yourself as an acknowledged expert in your field, then I have written this book to try to help you.

Don't get me wrong. It is not that I have any objection to having my books sell well or even making money from my writing. However, that is not my primary or even secondary purpose in writing and publishing the scholarship that I do. I am what I like to call a "legacy writer." That is, I write because I am in pursuit of making a significant and enduring contribution to my field of academic endeavor. In the course of this writing, I hope perhaps to discover some notions or ideas that others have not envisioned before, and maybe even leave an important permanent mark on my fields of study and research. I want future generations of scholars to still be picking up and profitably using the books and articles that I have written, because I captured something important in them, and not simply to find my (onetime popular) books remaindered or chucked out to make space in the library for the newest and latest publication. As a result, I personally focus on writing hard-core academic articles that appear in technical journals or books, and books in monograph series that mostly only academic libraries can afford.[1] The joke is that—and I hesitate to say this (and the publisher of this book should ignore what I am about to say)—I would have done all of the writing that I have done for absolutely no financial return, simply because I believe so strongly in the role and importance of making a meaningful scholarly contribution.

The most important reward that I have gained has been the repeated sense of accomplishment in pursuing a particular intellectual line through a maze of data until I have been able to craft a book or an article that has been accepted for publication and, when published, has become recognized as making a contribution to an ongoing debate, or perhaps even instigating a new area of research and discussion. I have been very fortunate in such regards, because I have become a recognized expert in a number of different fields or subfields, and have made worthwhile scholarly contributions in each of them. I have won awards for my writing and editing, and my first academic book is still in print and sells a reasonable number of copies each year. That book is something of a "best seller" in academic circles. When it first appeared in print, it was featured at a major scholarly conference by the publisher. It was 1989, and the publisher also published a book by the then pope of the Roman Catholic Church, John Paul II. That year, as I approached my publisher's display at this large conference, the publisher's representative took great pride in announcing loudly to everyone within earshot that "You, Stan, have outsold the pope." Too bad for the pope, because he was probably aiming at a wider and more popular audience than my book was, which was on ancient Greek verbal structure. Along the way as an active academic author, I have learned an awful lot about how to get into academic print.[2] Learning early on how to be a successful publishing author has certainly aided my academic career as I moved through the ranks from instructor to professor and even research professor, before becoming head of my own academic institution by the time I was forty-five. I also had the very good fortune to be the senior academic editor for a major international academic publishing company.[3] As a result, I have been asked by my students and others to share with them the inside story of my publishing success and have given lectures and workshops on this topic to students in research courses. So I have decided that, rather than keeping to myself many of the secrets of academic publishing that I have learned, or simply sharing them with my immediate students, I would write this book as a way of trying to help others who may wish to benefit from what I have often learned by experiment or trial and error. In this book, I am going to tell you everything I can think of that I have learned about how to be successful in academic publishing. I am not going to relate my comments to specific areas of academic endeavor any more than I believe is necessary. My experience of publishing in a number of fields has taught me that there are a number of substantial common principles that I can pass on that apply to any academic field. Most of these apply beyond simply biblical studies, theology and religion, and the arts and humanities—although I write with these areas primarily in mind.

This book is, to a large extent, an exercise in demystification and demythologizing. There is a lot of mythology that has come to be attached to the notion of publishing, and I—having penetrated beyond at least some, if not most, of it—will lay out everything that I have learned. I will reveal a number of secrets that the publishing industry, and especially the various editors in it, would probably prefer that I not tell. The ones who really do not want me to reveal what I am about to write are your fellow academics who would prefer to sit on the sidelines and enjoy their comfortable, nonpublishing academic lives. I assume that your picking up and reading this book indicates that you wish to move to the head of the pack in terms of publishing, and my intention is to help you to be able to do that on the basis of my own experience. The one thing that I ask you—besides recommending to your colleagues that they also buy a copy of this book—is that you take what I say seriously and consider it as a whole, even if some of it is not what you have heard from others before.

You may be surprised that I mentioned that one of the major opponents to what I have to say in this book is fellow academics. I know—because I have heard them say it—that there are some academics who recommend that young scholars not publish the results of their research for at least five years, or more. Some I have heard even recommend that young scholars hold off for fifteen years before they venture to put their major ideas into print. Besides the fact that by then you will no longer be young, I consider this to be terrible advice that should be ignored at all costs. In today's competitive academic climate, this is a virtual guarantee that your academic career never gets off the ground. I knew a colleague at one institution who had a Ph.D. from a very fine major university in a humanities subject.[4] Coming out of his doctoral program, he had thrown all of his attention into teaching, and he became a very popular and successful teacher of undergraduates. However, for whatever reason—possibly because he did not receive positive encouragement as is found in this book (as opposed to his receiving active discouragement)—he did no further scholarly research, and hence no publishing. He was holding out for his upcoming research leave. That research leave finally came, and he threw himself into it assiduously. However, when he came back to campus after being away, I had a chat with him. He told me that, because he had not engaged in scholarship in the years intervening between his doctorate and his research leave, when he went into the library to do research it was as if he had to start the academic process over again—it was like visiting a foreign country for the first time. He never recovered from his period of inactivity. The challenge of getting caught up and reactivating his scholarship was too great, and his research leave came to an end without his having produced a single publication, so far as I know.

By contrast, early on in my career, as I was developing my own research profile—we will talk more about this below—I had an ambitious junior-level undergraduate student who wanted to do some research in a particular area that was well beyond what was offered in a regular undergraduate course—or even graduate courses, for that matter. Over the span of a year, we worked together on his investigation of a particular linguistic conundrum. He concluded in his written paper that the standard explanation of this conundrum was incorrect, and that he had developed a more elegant explanation of the data. After a process of revision and refinement, I encouraged him to submit the paper for publication to one of the premier international journals in the field. My student's original draft cover letter said, to the effect, that he was a student who had been working on this particular problem, and he thought the journal would perhaps be interested in publishing it. I told him to go back and rewrite the letter, simply stating that he had been working on this particular problem and thought that the journal would be interested in his results. He sent the letter and manuscript to the publisher, and in due course it was accepted for publication without substantial revision, and it appeared as the lead article in the volume year. Not bad for an undergraduate in college. I met a senior colleague at a conference not too long after the article had appeared, and he commented on the recognizable quality of this article produced by one of my colleagues. When I pointed out to him that it was by one of my undergraduate students, he started to backtrack in his praise for the article. My only thought is that this had broken his paradigm of who is qualified to write groundbreaking articles. This book is designed to help others to break such paradigms and to develop a sustainable research profile that results in a publishing lifestyle.

About twenty years ago, when I signed a contract for a book with a well-known academic publisher, the contract had a statement that said that, at least for a period of time, this publisher was still committed to publishing printed books. The implication was that, after that period of time, the printed book as we know it may have disappeared. I have signed contracts with that publisher since, and I note that—at least for the time being—that clause is no longer there. For the foreseeable future, the academic book and article, published by recognized academic publishing companies and refereed journals, are here to stay. If you intend to make a contribution to academic publishing, then you will need to publish in these venues. Furthermore, publishers have to have enough material to publish and sell in order to stay in business—their business plans depend upon so many journals and/or books being published every year, year in and year out. This means that they have to publish so many volumes a year to pay their overhead, satisfy their shareholders or owners, and pay their salaries, and each fascicle of their journals must have enough articles in it to be published on time to keep to a schedule for billing purposes. The material they publish may as well be mine—and yours! This book is written to help you to make sure that this is the case.

1

📖

TYPES OF PUBLICATIONS

Like animals, as George Orwell would say,[1] not all types of publications
are equal. This became obvious to me and my academic colleagues when
I taught and headed a university-level department in London, England.
In the British educational system of the time, there was an enterprise
called the Research Assessment Exercise. The RAE, as it was popularly
labeled, was a nationally conducted exercise during which various university research units, organized by subject area, were evaluated in terms of
the quantity and quality of their published research. The RAE took place
every four to six years, and each assessed unit submitted both selective
lists and the actual publications for their contributors so that they could
be evaluated. An expert assessment panel for each subject area had the
daunting task over the course of the best part of a year of actually sitting down and reading through the submissions and evaluating both each
individual (this information was kept confidential) and then each unit of
assessment on the basis of a scale, from best to worst. The top rating was
reserved for those departments that, on the basis of the concrete evidence
of the publications of the individuals within it, warranted international
standing, the next place for those with national standing, on down to
those having essentially no scholarly standing.

This research assessment process had a number of tangible and
serious implications. One of the most obvious was in terms of funding
for research. Dependent upon the government funds available, units or
departments that received a certain rating or above were given extra
research funding on the basis of a formula that took into account the
number of submitted scholars in the unit and the amount given for that
particular rating. A second implication, and perhaps more important than

the funding, as valuable as that was, was the bragging rights that attached to success in the exercise. There were league tables created for each subject area, and then, on the basis of those league tables and other factors, ratings were given to all of the universities throughout Britain.[2]

The preparation for this exercise was intense, the competition fierce, and the sense of relief when it was over only temporarily mitigated, as the next exercise was already being planned. The rating system was not perfect, and of course there were politics involved, but the entire exercise helped to focus your attention on research and publication in a variety of ways. During the time that I participated in the exercise, a given individual was to submit their entire list of publications for the period under assessment, and designate their four most important publications to be specifically evaluated as the basis of the individual and then the unit rating. This meant that, during the course of the four or more years to be assessed, each scholar had to identify a number of meritorious projects to get written and published in time to be entered before the cutoff date for submission of entries. So who disliked the RAE the most? Of course, it was those who did not publish very much or at all—or those who were always talking about the great magnum opus ("big work" sounds better in Latin, doesn't it) they were working on that would no doubt one day appear and change both the discipline and the world. Most of those works never appeared. Scholars who thrived in such an exercise were those who had a pattern of publishing already established, and who had a clear idea of which publications counted the most in the grand scheme of academic publishing.

In this chapter, I will lay out my scale and the relative merits of the different types of publications available for those in biblical studies, theology and religion, and the arts and humanities. This scale may not be universally applicable to each specific discipline or subdiscipline within those fields (some of the fields allow practical or performance projects), but, on the basis of my experience, it is universal enough that it holds true for the vast majority of areas. We do not have an exercise equivalent to the RAE in North America by which to judge academic departments and institutions—I won't comment on whether I think it is a good idea or not, except to say that it is far more objective than simply asking the opinion of your dean or head of department regarding another institution—but that does not mean that the various types of publications available to scholars cannot be categorized on the basis of their relative weight and prestige. They can, and you should know what they are and how they are viewed, as a means of helping to determine where you will spend your publication efforts.

To be blunt and to the point, the nature, type, and number of publications in recognized monograph series and prestigious refereed journals are what truly establish a research profile. A research profile essentially means that you, as a scholar, have defined for yourself your academic interests and your areas of expertise, and have proven it through serious, peer-recognized publications. This profile is then recognized by others. If your profile is defined sufficiently well by publishing in the right series, journals, and even collections of essays, you will become identified with this particular subject area. Besides being recognized by other scholars as an expert in your particular area, the practical results of such identification are several. Sometimes it can result in opportunities being extended to you to make a further contribution in that area. Sometimes it is a journal, other times a monograph series, sometimes a conference or a reference work, that needs a contribution in a particular area. If you have a research profile in this area, you may well be asked to contribute to such a topic of research. I recommend that you say "yes" to virtually all these opportunities if you are serious about making an impact. An active research and publishing profile keeps your interest in the subject current, it shows to others that you are interested in continuing to be a contributor to that field, and it helps to form connections for other work that you may be doing. A number of years ago I wrote a monograph on a particular area of personal interest, and one where I held a distinct minority position. Since that book appeared, I have been repeatedly invited to make further contributions on the topic. These opportunities have included appointment to the editorial board of a journal, and invitations to give papers (sometimes expenses paid) in places ranging from Princeton to Prague.

A second practical result is that an active research profile may pave the way for you to publish in the area without having to constantly re-prove yourself to the editors or publishers involved. If you are the person identified with the subject, you may have easier access to publication in the area. As a result of my establishing a research profile in a particular area, editors of standard reference tools in my primary areas of research have asked me to provide conspectuses of these subjects. Each one gives me a chance to get caught up on the latest research in the area and even extend the discussion.

There are a number of different ways of talking about the kinds of publications that a scholar might pursue in establishing a research profile. I select seven here and rank them in general descending order of importance, insofar as scholarly weight and prestige are concerned (the one exception is the edited volume, which appears after authored books and monographs). In this chapter, I cover the following types of publications: (1) books and monographs; (2) edited volumes; (3) articles in journals, both refereed and unrefereed; (4) chapters in collections of essays; (5) dictionary and encyclopedia articles; (6) book reviews; and (7) papers for conferences and other invitations.

Books and Monographs

Rumors of the book's demise, to paraphrase Mark Twain, are greatly exaggerated. More books are published each year than ever before. Even though a number of academic publishers have got themselves into financial trouble,[3] despite these difficulties the academic monograph still holds sway. For most disciplines within biblical studies, theology and religion, and the arts and humanities, the authored or coauthored monograph or original research volume has the highest standing in the profession and continues to be the gold standard. Some subdisciplines may emphasize journal articles for their timeliness, but there is something sufficiently and obviously serious about a book that it is still given pride of place by some distance.

There is sometimes a rough and ready distinction made between a monograph and other types of books. In the world of trade publishing (for popular consumption, and not for academic purposes), there are a number of types of books that are produced—trade paperbacks, hardbacks, and the like. Sometimes these books are focused on a general academic topic, but they mostly include a wide range of subjects and approaches that fall outside of the monograph. As this book (or is this a monograph?) is concerned with academic publishing, I am mostly concerned with what is usually called the academic monograph. However, I will often use the term "book" interchangeably, as well as including other types of book-length writing projects.

There are several key considerations regarding the academic book or monograph that are worth considering in contemplating writing and publishing one.

Specific Focus

The first element is that the monograph needs to be specifically focused. This means that the monograph must have more than simply a topic in mind that unites the material together—it must argue for a particular thesis or idea that unites the content so that the volume makes a clear and forceful statement regarding that thesis. A subject or topic is what a book is about, and includes such things as New Testament prophecy, sixteenth-century English choral music, French verbal structure, Shakespeare's tragedies, and the like. A thesis or thesis statement articulates what you wish to say about your subject. Thus, my thesis might be that New Testament prophecy continues the prophetic tradition of the Old Testament because of its invocation of the notion of God speaking, or that sixteenth-century English choral music marked a significant turning point in the development of polyphonic music, or that French verbal structure is not time-based but aspectual, or that Shakespeare's tragedies epitomize his jaundiced view of Elizabethan court life.[4] Whatever the thesis, the volume needs to focus upon this statement, marshal the necessary evidence, and bring the various strands together to make as convincing a point as possible. A good dissertation submitted for a Ph.D. degree, and even sometimes for an M.A., should provide the makings for a good monograph.

Research Level and Citation

The monograph needs to reflect the appropriate level of research and type of citation to support the nature of the volume that it is. Each discipline has its own conventions and level of research documentation, but one of the hallmarks of the monograph is that it must reflect an appropriate level of research. How this research is displayed often varies from discipline to discipline. There are a number of subjects, such as English literature, where a minimal amount of documentation from secondary literature is quite normal and acceptable. There are other subjects, such as biblical studies, where the discipline has developed to the point that documentation of secondary literature is often quite heavy and intense, with a wide use of citation and content footnotes.[5] There are other disciplines that fall somewhere in between. Most of the arts, humanities, and theology/religion disciplines have used a traditional method of footnoting or endnoting, so that the documentation is presented in full form for other scholars to check. Some of these disciplines, however, have come to welcome social science (sometimes called Harvard-style) referencing. In most cases, these references consist of the author's name, the date of publication, and usually (though not always) a page number,[6] with a bibliography of works cited at the end of the manuscript, organized so that the author's name and the date are obvious. These social-scientific style citations are virtually all citation notes, as they give direct attribution to the source of a quotation, opinion, or other piece of information derived from another scholar. Content footnotes are more difficult with this style, as they are used for secondary discussions that do not merit inclusion within the body of the text. The proper method to use depends upon the academic discipline and the requirements of the publication—usually not the personal preference of the author, regardless of how strongly you may hold to such a position.

More important than the style of citation is the level of research itself. Some disciplines require close argumentation throughout an article or monograph, while others require a more narrative accounting in the text, with appropriate documentation in the notes, while still others simply want a clear accounting of the basic ideas. These various levels of research are also dictated by the subject matter and the type of publication within the discipline concerned. A close reading of an ancient Latin document, such as one might find in a textual commentary, might require a detailed treatment of philological and related linguistic issues, while a discussion of a modern novel might require less attention to individual words and much more summary discussion of the unfolding of the plot and the nature of the characters. In any case, the level of research is often indicated by the nature of the discipline, the subject matter, and even the requirements and style of the publisher.

Authorship and Coauthorship

A third element is the issue of authorship itself. Most monographs are single-authored works; however, there is also the opportunity occasionally for multiauthored monographs. I have written several monographs with other scholars. Publishers will often tell you that coauthored works do not sell as well as single-authored monographs (their reasons for this may not be entirely altruistic, as some factors may be more complex for the publisher, such as handling author relations and paying of royalties), but that simply tells you what the priority of far too many publishers is—

money. If the book comes about as a result of coauthorship, or is a better book because of it, then coauthorship is not just an acceptable idea but a good idea to pursue. I have found that the challenge of working with another author is one of the best ways to create authorial accountability. Coauthorship builds in project or writing accountability so that we meet the deadlines that we have set for the project, and it builds in authorial accountability because we have another trusted and expert reader to test what we have written before it goes any further in the publication process.

I would encourage scholars to coauthor monographs with others, for several reasons. One is that coauthorship allows authors to expand their horizons in appropriate ways. I may be an expert on premodern poetry and my colleague an expert on modern poetry. Together we may be able to write a book on poetry that competently addresses poetry from premodern to modern times, rather than one of us addressing an area that we are not expert in and not doing as good a job. Another reason is that coauthorship can result in producing more scholarship in less time, because the burden of writing is being shared. If I can coauthor a volume with a friend, we can produce two books in roughly the amount of time that it takes to produce one volume—in fact, in less time, if the coauthorship forces us to meet deadlines that might otherwise be missed if we were simply writing on our own. A third reason is that coauthorship can force us to explore new intellectual and academic areas that we might not otherwise be drawn to. I was approached by a colleague with the opportunity to write a broad-ranging advanced-level textbook.[7] I was not at the place in my career when I thought I wanted to do such a project, especially because it would force me to say something about just about everything in the field, and I was not yet ready to do so on my own. However, because my colleague would write half the book, I could write on the parts that I was prepared to write on. The result was a substantial textbook that we both shared in producing, even though we were probably not equally expert in each area. I am very proud of the product of this collaboration. Lastly, the process of thinking through and developing a jointly authored project alone can often make for a much improved final product.

Compositional Methods

I have been surprised in talking with other scholars about how intimidating it can often be for a scholar to contemplate writing and publishing a monograph. It does not need to be that difficult. The simple model for such a project is for you first to define a thesis statement that you wish to explore. Perhaps you wish to prove that the Apostle Paul authored the book of 2 Thessalonians, or that Shakespeare's early tragedies are stylistically more cohesive than are his later ones, or that Matthew's Gospel was written before Mark's. In any case, you need to develop this thesis statement in sufficient detail and then construct a plan for developing the argument to prove the point. The major stages in this argument are usually the chapters of the volume. The writing of the monograph then becomes simply the task of treating each individual unit—usually a chapter—as an extended essay on that particular part of the overall topic.

This is the straightforward approach, but there are others as well. There have been occasions when a scholar has been prompted by a previously written essay to write on a particular topic. Perhaps the scholar has written a journal article on Shakespeare's *Macbeth* and now wishes to pursue the wider issue of Shakespeare's tragedies. It may be possible to incorporate the work that has been done for the particular scholarly essay as part of the final monograph. Depending on how much of the previous essay is used, and how much writing and rewriting of the essay is done, you will probably need to contact the editor or publisher of the journal or volume of essays that published the original piece for permission to reuse it.[8] There are also occasions when it is legitimate for you to develop a monograph out of a collection of several previously published essays, so long as you can weave a suitable focused theme through these essays. The key is for you to ensure that the reader sees how the individual essays fit together to support the major thesis that is being argued. Often a lengthy and detailed opening chapter is what is needed to ensure that the major threads are tied together throughout the ensuing chapters.

You might wonder whether the publisher of the essay mentioned above may choose not to allow reuse of the essay, or even want to charge you, the author, for reuse of your own essay! The standard, though not invariable, practice is for the journal or publisher of the collection of chapters to own the copyright to the particular essays, although some authors retain the copyright themselves for such an eventuality as this. Usually publishers—and certainly the best ones—are more than willing to allow reuse of an essay, and you should record somewhere in the resultant book where the essay was originally published, giving full and complete publishing information. This can occur in a preface or list of previous publications, or as a footnote at the appropriate place in the monograph itself. Publishers should provide this permission freely and without charge to the original author of the essay—after all, it is your work that you are asking to reuse. In many, if not most, academic areas, authors are not paid very much if anything for an essay to appear in an edited collection of essays, and virtually always nothing in scholarly journals, so it only seems right and fair to allow authors to reuse their own work. Occasionally a publisher will try to charge for use, but they should be able to be convinced otherwise, especially if you are an author whom they want to publish again. It can even happen that a publisher will deny permission for use. I was refused once by a publisher. My response was simply to scratch that publisher off my list of those I would publish with again. There are plenty of other publishers available, so there is no need to despair.

Incidentally, there are other ways of making use of previously published material, and that is by essentially creating a new piece of work. An author, for example, can rewrite, supplement, expand or contract, and otherwise alter the material so significantly that the essay is essentially a new essay, or at least changed enough that it qualifies as a new essay.[9] In this way, you make use of your previous research, as well as taking account of any responses you received to your original publication, producing in effect a new treatment of the subject, with your best thoughts recast in terms of further research and reflection. Be cautious if you ever hear of a publisher going after an academic author for doing something like this. Remember that academic publishers are heavily dependent upon authors to stay in business—they are dependent upon us for the books that they publish and the articles that they put in their journals, so they cannot get a reputation for being litigious or unreasonable with their authors, or they simply will not have their authors' favor, or articles and books, any longer.

Monographs and the Research Profile

A fifth—tangential, yet important—issue concerns how many monographs a scholar should produce in order to establish a research profile. This is a difficult question to answer, because it depends on the subject area, the competitiveness of the discipline, the quality of the monographs, and the like, but my general recommendation is that a scholar needs a minimum of two monographs in a subject area to establish subject-specific expertise. I was once asked to assess a fellow scholar for promotion. While I noted that she had several reasonably weighty and significant monographs published, as well as other works, I also observed that each one was in a different subject area, and so it was difficult for me to determine the area in which she had established her expertise. Note that I said that I believe that *two or more published monographs* in an area are necessary.

Some time ago I heard through the scholarly grapevine that a colleague of mine was complaining to a friend that it was difficult to pin down my area of expertise, because I had published so much. I thought that this comment sounded petty, but it does raise the question of assessing one's area of expertise. I went back and examined my publications and noted that, in at least two areas, I had at least as many, if not more, monographs (as well as supporting journal articles and chapters in volumes) in each major area than the critical scholar had published in his entirety. I dismissed his petty comments but took note to ensure that in the future I would try to publish two or more monographs in each area that I wished to claim as an area of expertise.[10]

I have written a number of different types of technical, academic monographs, with each type of variation on the monograph form having its own particular merit. My first was an edited version of my doctoral thesis and hence was a highly detailed technical treatise, full of references to secondary literature, but also arguing a new and—at the time (the major thesis has now been widely accepted in the discipline)— challenging hypothesis. Another monograph was based in small part on a master's thesis that I wrote but then greatly expanded so that the M.A. thesis was basically contained in only a couple of chapters, or parts of chapters. I have also written a monograph that draws together a number of previously published papers that are recast so as to argue a sustained thesis, and another that draws on a couple of previously published papers and a number of previously unpublished conference papers and that puts forward a new hypothesis. One of my monographs was inspired by a single paper that I was asked to write for a conference (the paper was never published, due to unforeseen difficulties) but that was developed into an entire technical volume. I have also collaborated on several volumes, with a number of different coauthors. In all of these collaborative instances, as I have indicated above, I have tried to work with someone who complements my expertise, so that we can cover the subject better together than either of us could alone. These volumes differ in length, format, and style, but they all attempt to argue for a specific thesis.

Assessment of Significance

Various types of publications carry various weights insofar as scholarly significance, prestige, and even practical usefulness in such a thing as tenure review are concerned. In assessing the relative weight of a monograph with regard to other recognized forms of publication, I use the factor of five as a general rule of thumb. In other words, I count a monograph, whether authored or coauthored, as worth five units, or five times the value of an article in a refereed journal or a significant chapter in a collection of essays. If you examine the average monograph, it probably has more than five chapters in it, and quite probably is longer than five times the average length of a journal article. However, the monograph is focused on a single subject and so does not require the same amount of research time as five separate articles, each of which often requires tackling a new subject area. In establishing the life of a writing scholar (see chapter 9 below, where I propose a method for calculating your research productivity), these figures are worth keeping in mind to plan the kind of production that will establish a suitable research profile.

Other Book Types

Besides the technical monograph, there are other types of books that have varying degrees of scholarly merit, some of which have been noted above. These include handbooks to a field of study, textual and related commentaries, annotated bibliographies that survey the secondary research in a discipline, textbooks, and popular summaries of a field, among others that one can imagine. Each of these has some merit in its own right, even if they don't all carry the same amount of weight as a technical monograph, or make the same lasting or significant contribution to an area of academic study.

Textbooks that are simply scaled down or toned down treatments of a subject without scholarly apparatus do not carry much weight in academic publishing—although huge numbers of them are sold and they often make their authors lots of money. The money is often generated by the need to come out with new editions of the book every couple of years, in order to keep the book up to date and—the overriding reason—to keep your publisher ahead of the rival publisher attempting to promote a similar textbook in the same field. The textbooks that I have in mind here serve a very valuable role in introducing beginning students to a subject, but they are usually addressed to the novice and cannot by definition step out into new academic or intellectual territory. As a result, they contribute little to nothing new to the discipline and hence cannot be considered on the same level as a scholarly monograph. One way around this dilemma is to write a book that is not written specifically as a textbook (i.e., it does not cover all areas of the subject, and there are no study questions or the like included) but that could still be adopted as a class text (required or supplemental reading). This volume will have to ensure that it actually makes a new contribution to the field and has suitable scholarly apparatus to show that the author is not simply shooting from the hip of accepted opinion. I mentioned above the coauthored textbook that I wrote with a colleague so that we could cover the range of the subject without each of us having to master the entire field. This book was written as a textbook, but it included much more than most textbooks in the field.[11] Our book included a more comprehensive view of the subject, thus obviating the need to purchase two textbooks, as is often the case in this field. Along the way and at various points, each of us included material that reflected our unique perspectives on the material.

Of more academic worth than textbooks are handbooks and anno-tated bibliographies. A well-done handbook makes a contribution to the field because it offers a conspectus of opinion but goes further in evaluat-ing this opinion and making positive suggestions. Such handbooks often address students who are at a more advanced level, or even scholars who want an introduction to a field that is new to them or that they have not studied for some time but with which they want to become reacquainted or in which they wish to be informed of the latest thinking. I have written a book of this sort—an intermediate-level treatment of the Greek lan-guage that has, incidentally, served as a useful textbook in many second-year and advanced-level Greek courses. What distinguishes this book is that it incorporates some of the cutting-edge thinking in my earlier monograph on Greek verbal structure, as well as introducing a number of other concepts into treatment of a subject that must cover certain issues if it is going to prove useful as an intermediate-level handbook on the Greek language. The annotated bibliography is a much-neglected type of work, because it requires a broad range of knowledge while not allowing the author to argue a sustained thesis. However, annotated bibliographies often provide very valuable guidance, because they have reached into many of the nooks and crannies of a discipline in search of significant past research that has often gone neglected or passed out of fashion. In this sense, a good bibliographer can have an impact on a field by bringing back into play significant past work now ignored. (And I am a great believer in the value of this.)

In closing this section, let me mention a regrettable downward spiral occurring in some academic areas. The unfortunate movement is the inclination to downgrade a subject area to the level of popular interest, either as part of a career move or in response to populist (and monetary?) pressures. In many fields, there is a tendency for a young scholar to make an initial academic contribution and then to revert soon after to publishing popular-level treatments of the subject. There are, of course, some justifiable reasons for writing popular works of this sort, but much of the time it marks the passing of a point of no return regarding serious scholarship. A series of popular treatments, one after another, can easily result in a scholar becoming a popularizer, and serious and lasting scholarship is the victim. The justification that the "person on the street" needs high-quality exposure to such work is no justification at all when we notice that such curiosity is never satisfied but always demands more such treatments, not for knowledge's sake (otherwise intellectual levels would be elevated) but simply out of prurient interest. Another consequence is that it is often hard for such a person to make the hard return to scholarly research, to say nothing of the time and effort wasted on such ephemeral publications. Such publications often do not even stay in print long enough to be reviewed, and even if they are, they appeal to the lowest common level of knowledge and do not advance scholarship. I must admit that I have written several popular volumes. It is wonderful to have the adulation and recognition that often accompany such efforts—one such book of mine was sold for movie rights and made into a documentary for public television!—but this is to be cursed by the commonplace. Certainly such efforts should not be encouraged or rewarded by such things as tenure or scholarly recognition.

The Monograph and the Agent

A word should be said about an unfortunate trend in publishing that has potential (and already determinable) deleterious effects on all of scholarship. This involves the tendency for some publishers to no longer accept unsolicited proposals or manuscripts. These publishers, for whatever reason—and I am not convinced that there is a good one, only their desire to save their own time and energy so as to make more money—have decided that they are so far above their potential authors that they will not be in communication with them. Instead, an author who wishes to approach such a publishing house is required to do so through a recognized literary agent.[12] There are clear reasons why this trend has developed, such as the growing number of people who consider themselves "authors" when they shouldn't, the need to place marketing at the core of the publishing industry, and the lack of expertise by publishers to judge the range of manuscripts that they are sent. There are a number of problems here. For one, it is increasingly rare that commissioning editors for publishing companies are as competent in their respective fields as the authors that they are wishing to publish. In fact, it is an increasingly rare publishing company, especially the commercial and nonacademic houses, in my experience, that has commissioning or other editors with Ph.D.'s and sometimes even master's degrees in the technical fields. These publishers and their editors may know a lot about selling books (I say "may," as I am not always convinced even of this), but they sometimes have very little significant knowledge of the subjects that they publish.[13] In any event, even if they did, the solution is not to isolate themselves even further from authors by requiring the services of agents as intermediaries and first filters. I am familiar with a number of agents, and I am sure that some of them are very good. However, my impression of many of them is similar to my thoughts about some of the editors and publishing companies. Some of these agents are former employees of publishing companies as acquisitions editors or copy editors or whatever, some have worked in the retail book trade, and others have a variety of other types of experience. Few of them are actually academics, and those that are authors usually write at the popular level, without really understanding scholarship. This compounding of academic ignorance undermines academic publishing.

I have seen the results of this unfortunate process firsthand. At one point, I was in contact with an agent because I was wondering whether she would be of help to me in increasing the scope of my publishing beyond academic work. Subsequently, I discovered that any of the publishers that I would have wanted to publish with were available to me by one means or another without an agent. However, I learned that this agent would only consider representing me if she could represent all of my book proposals, including my academic books. She would not do so, however, until she could scrutinize a complete book manuscript. Now let me see what this means. I have been able to place with respectable publishers every book manuscript that I have written, and now this agent wants to come along to tell me—if she deigns to represent me—what I should and shouldn't write, and take a hefty percentage of my royalties—15–20 percent—for projects I could easily arrange myself? Needless to say, I am not using an agent. To be fair, with or without an agent running interference, academic publishers still have some problems in determining what they should be publishing. I once made inquiries of a major academic publisher regarding their publishing a very famous ancient manuscript. Even if such a publishing venture would not be a huge moneymaker for the publisher—whose books often are very highly priced anyway—it would have garnered high praise and prestige. Kudos in the book world are very valuable to publishers. My conversation with an acquisitions editor in the subject area left me with the distinct impression that the editor did not even recognize the manuscript I was talking about, had no knowledge of their or any other publishers' previous connection with such a project, and, in any case, was not interested in this proposal. So much for publishers recognizing the potential quality of publications. But don't despair at agents' and publishers' unconscionable ignorance. I will address this issue in several chapters below.

The Monograph and the Advance Royalty

In recent times, some authors—no doubt encouraged by avarice, whether promoted by agents or not—have begun regularly to demand large advance royalties in anticipation of publication.[14] An agent will hypothetically approach a publisher and say that a certain author—who is, of course, in the agent's humble and unbiased opinion, the best since Shakespeare—is taking bids for his next monograph. The publisher, not wanting to miss out on this exciting, never to be repeated (until the next book) opportunity, calculates what kind of an advance might be possible in light of (usually exaggerated) anticipated sales of the book. Of course, the advance offered is not—in probably the great majority of instances— even close to what the author or agent claims to have been anticipating, and the publisher, not wanting to be outdone, increases the offered advance. In all too many cases, so it seems, the book that arrives from the author does not live up to the highly touted expectations, and the sales are even worse. The result is that the publisher ends up losing significant amounts of money on the book. Not only is the publisher the victim, but so are the authors of other books who now cannot be published by this publisher because the publisher has no money left for books that may be of better quality but by less well-known or less well-advocated authors.

Who is to blame in this situation? All three parties, it is sad to say, are clearly to blame. Authors are to blame for being downright greedy and so enamored of themselves that they think that their work is of such value and popularity—even when it is not—that it merits publication even though it creates a cash flow problem for the publisher. In one recent case, in a public venue at a scholarly conference, an author was bragging that his advance on a recent book had provided so much money that he could buy his wife a new car. The comments were not about the contribution of the book or its crucial argument, but its cash value. I suggest to authors who have such high ambitions to get another line of work, where they have a more realistic and humble view of their abilities. Better yet, I suggest that they get a decent-paying academic job that enables them to write whatever they want and to publish it even if there are no royalties attached—simply for the love of the subject and the contribution that they can make to it.

The agents are to blame too. These guardians of the doors may not be engaging in out-and-out lying but certainly seem on occasion to come close to prevarication and duplicity. Not having seen a manuscript, they have no basis for saying whether this is the best book since, well, the last blockbuster they tried to sell. If they have seen it and know that it is not the greatest, then they are being deceptive. (Even if they have seen it, do they really have an idea of whether it is good or not?)

The publishers, however, must also shoulder a good portion of the blame. All that they need to do, as the old advertising campaign used to say, is "just say no." A publisher may lose out on the occasional best seller, but creating one's financial plan around the expectation of publishing a best seller every year or two is hardly a responsible business plan for long-term sustainability. Several publishers have recently learned this lesson the hard way—with jobs being lost as a result. Instead, publishing books that make contributions to the field, even if they do not sell overwhelming amounts but enough copies to stay in business and provide a fair royalty to authors (and perhaps nothing to such agents as depicted above), is a method for sustainable publishing.

Related to the issue of submitting a proposal to the publisher is that of the review of the proposal or manuscript by the publisher. I say more about refereeing such proposals below, in my section on journal articles.

There are many monographs published. Some of the best monographs are the first books published by their respective authors, often a revised form of a dissertation. Very few monographs make the kind of sustained and abiding impact that their authors or publishers desire. However, good monographs are readily recognizable by the quality of their argument, the depth of their analysis, the scope of their research, and the implications they have for fostering further research. Good monographs, rather than bringing discussion to a close, raise the right kinds of questions that promote further productive research.

Edited Volumes

Another form of book is the edited volume of individual essays or chapters by various authors, or even all chapters by the same author. I include edited volumes in their own section, not for the academic credit that they garner for the editor of the volume but because of their contribution as a whole to academia. The editing task itself, while requiring foresight, organization, conceptual planning, and technical abilities, and though often difficult and requiring a set of personal skills in order to cajole articles and corrections out of recalcitrant authors, does not itself contribute to the body of knowledge of a field. Despite this significant limitation, the value of editing volumes is immense for four good reasons.[15]

Contribution to Knowledge

One of the primary reasons for editing a volume is that the volume itself can, either in terms of individual essays or as a whole, make a contribution to the academic discipline. There are certain subjects for which defining the field in a monograph may be difficult, or the state of play of a discipline may be such that a monograph is not appropriate, or the current circumstances may warrant something other than a sustained work by an individual scholar. In such cases, an edited volume may be the perfect venue for disparate opinions to be aired side by side. Perhaps as a result, there will be a critical mass of interest generated to advance the field to the point of needing and requiring monographs. In this way, the editing of volumes can have a formative and directional influence upon a discipline.

More Voices

Edited volumes provide opportunities for an increased number of scholars to be participants, and hence for multiple voices and opinions to be heard on a topic. There are few subjects that cannot benefit from hearing a range of differing opinions. Perhaps some scholars do not believe that they have enough to say to warrant a monograph, but they may well have enough to say to write an excellent chapter in a collection of essays. Other scholars may be new to an area of investigation and wish to try out an idea or approach before committing themselves to an entire monograph. The occasion of the edited collection might well help to start or restart the publishing career of a colleague by providing a manageable publishing goal, rather than demanding an entire monograph.

Collaborative Opportunities

The editing of a volume of essays is an excellent opportunity for collaboration. The contents of the collection can come about from any number of possible sources. A defined conference on a select topic is an excellent source for papers in a collection, but collections can also be formed simply around an interesting idea. You as the editor have the opportunity to invite the contributors of your choice. Some of these contributors might be people already known to you, while others might be those whom you wish to get to know. The occasion of planning a volume such as this gives the opportunity to make contact with scholars in a way that invites further contact. Collections of essays can also come about from previously published essays, perhaps those that are formative for a discipline or reflect crucial turning points or transitions in the discipline, or even give honor to a particularly significant scholar in a field of study.

Editor's Contribution

Editing a collection provides an opportunity for the editor to contribute to the field, perhaps even a field in which the editor claims no specialist expertise. I would recommend that, except on the rare occasion, you as an editor of a volume try to contribute at least one substantive essay to a collection. Usually this will mean a significant essay on the topic of the collection, although it might also include an introductory chapter that itself makes a unique contribution in the way that it frames the topic of the volume and the essays that are included. If the topic of the volume is not one that you consider an area of research specialty, contributing to the volume provides an opportunity to become familiar with a new field of study. This might in itself open up new possibilities. Thomas Kuhn observed that those who make significant contributions to fields of study are often those who are new to a field or are young in age and outlook, because they have not had all of the definitive answers drilled into them. Instead, they come new and fresh to a discipline and don't know that they are not supposed to ask certain questions or take particular approaches.[16] Editing a volume of essays on a new topic provides potential for an illuminating situation in which the editor comes to the subject with a fresh and potentially insightful perspective. This may open up for you entirely new avenues of research.

I have edited over fifty-five volumes, often in collaboration with a coeditor. Some of these collections have been composed of previously published essays, such as essays from a particularly important journal. I coedited seven volumes with a friend, gathering what we considered the best essays on a series of topics published in a well-known journal over the course of ten years. Other edited volumes have come about as a result of conferences that I have regularly helped to organize, or in which I have had a supervisory role. I have organized or coorganized roughly a conference a year over the last fifteen years, and often I have assembled an edited volume of essays from each conference. On some occasions, I have gathered essays from several different conferences held over several years, to assemble a single edited volume of papers. Still other edited volumes have come about as the result of simply having an idea for a volume. My first coedited volume was completed under the supervision of a senior scholar who guided his two junior editors in assembling a volume of commemorative essays. This process taught us how to write to potential authors, graciously accept their rejection of our tremendous proposal, find other authors, set deadlines, edit essays, send off the compiled manuscript to the publisher, and then read proofs and compile indexes—all of which tasks are covered in this book below.

This is probably the best place to say something about the edited volume of essays that is put together to honor another scholar. The German word *Festschrift* is often used for such volumes. At a significant milestone in a scholar's career, usually a former colleague or student honors a senior scholar by editing a collection of essays by other scholars. These volumes are particularly tricky, because the unifying factor is usually not a topic, theme, or subject but simply the person. As a result, the collection of essays is often quite disparate and varied, both in subject and in quality. I once had lunch with a well-known scholar (with a sardonic sense of humor) who described *Festschriften* as volumes in which scholars "give of their second best." In other words, often scholars are contacted by the editor and asked for a contribution, not because they are writing in a particular area, but simply because they have some level of contact with this well-known scholar who is retiring, turning sixty years old, or the like. They may send in a paper that has no other immediate place of publication. As a result, a number of publishers do not readily accept *Festschriften*, because they are notoriously poor sellers.

I think that *Festschriften* are an important contribution to the scholarly arena of books because they represent the history of a given discipline as it is passed from one generation to another. There are also often hidden gems to be found in the essays. Nevertheless, there are a number of factors to consider here if you wish to get a *Festschrift* accepted for publication, as many publishers steer well clear of them. One is to try to get the best-quality essays possible, by the best scholars. There is no honor to a scholar in putting together a collection of third-rate contributions by third-rate scholars—even if they all think that he was a great guy! Publishers prefer to see a list of potential contributors who have made a contribution to the field in their own right. A second factor is to consider a specific focus for the *Festschrift*. A number of *Festschriften* have appeared recently that have directed the contributors to focus upon a topic or theme that is identified with the recipient. Thus, you might ask contributors to write on issues related to the Italian sonnet, even if the sonnet was only one area in which this distinguished professor of Romance languages was interested. This approach gives the volume focus, but it does run the risk of excluding some contributors who simply are not willing or able to contribute on that topic. A third factor is to find an academic publisher who is not as dependent upon high sales, such as a publisher who sells mostly to libraries, and who is more interested in a volume of good essays, and then approach that publisher. Your *Festschrift* in honor of Professor Jones, retiring professor of arcane languages, probably won't be sold in Barnes & Noble, but it will be published and honor the recipient.

As noted above, the editing of a volume in itself does not contribute value to one's research profile, except for any research contribution that might be included in such a volume. Only an unwise editor, however, would not exercise some editorial control over the quality of the essays included in a volume that he or she was producing. Even though the scholarly position and views of an article should reflect back upon the individual author who makes the case, it is unavoidable that there will be fallout or collateral damage for all involved in the project, and especially the editor, if the volume has too many essays that fail to meet up to the standards of the rest of the essays or what the subject matter and academic field demand, or are poorly presented and edited. There are two types of editors in this regard: interventionist and noninterventionist editors. Interventionist editors exercise strong editorial control over any essay that they publish in such a collection, going so far as to strongly edit the writing itself. Noninterventionist editors correct matters of fact, spelling errors, and clear grammatical infelicities, while letting the individual authors take responsibility for the chapters that appear under their names. I tend to be a noninterventionist editor. Besides it taking less time and hence leaving more time for other projects, I do not believe that interventionist editing actually significantly improves the final product. A colleague told me of his experience with a highly interventionist editor whom we will name Frank. As my colleague said regarding his completely rewritten essay, "I don't know if the rewritten essay was any better, but it sure sounded a lot more like Frank." My goal as editor is to let authors sound as much like themselves as I can.

The value of individual essays is discussed below. However, the compensation for the editor is that, by producing such a volume, the editor is contributing to the research profile of others, and perhaps through that, promoting the general advancement of the discipline, possibly even publishing that rare chapter that shapes an entire discipline.

Articles in Journals—Refereed and Unrefereed

The bread and butter of most scholarly careers, at least in the early years, is the refereed journal article. The journal article is an article of almost any size—from a one page note to an eighty page near (small) monograph—that is released in a publication that appears regularly or periodically. Scholarly journals are published with varying degrees of frequency, and their individual fascicles are of varying lengths as well. It is not uncommon for journals to appear two or four times a year, although some are released only once and some three times. There are some journals that are published even more often than four times in a given year. Each of the individual fascicles of a volume year of a journal will probably have a consistent size, so that when all of them are bound together the journal approximates the same size each volume year. The regularity of appearance of these journals allows plenty of opportunity for scholarly publication.

The Difference between Refereed and Unrefereed Books and Articles

One of the most fundamental and basic issues to discuss is the difference between a refereed and an unrefereed book manuscript or journal article. To say it simply and plainly, one of the greatest myths in publishing is the notion of the validity and value of the peer-reviewed article or book manuscript. There is an unfortunate tendency to believe that because an article (or book) has been peer reviewed it is of inherently higher quality than an unrefereed book or article. This may be true in the broadest of terms, but the situation is not quite as sanguine as some—especially editors, deans, and heads of tenure committees—would want others to believe. The first fact to realize is that the referees for such proposals are people just like you and me. I have been a peer reviewer for any number of publishing companies, a regular reviewer as a member of the editorial boards of a number of monograph series, an occasional reviewer for articles submitted to a variety of journals, a regular member of a number of journal editorial boards, and an editor of both monograph series and journals. I have no idea how many manuscripts of various types I have reviewed or had reviewed, but it is no doubt in the hundreds, if not over a thousand. Don't get me wrong, whenever I am asked to review an article, I do my best to give an opinion on its suitability for publication in that particular journal or by that particular publisher, and I expect those I ask to review to do the same thing. However, I am also happy to admit that I am a human being with a particular orientation to my subject, beliefs regarding what is and is not good scholarship, and even prejudices—yes, it's true!—regarding certain positions in these fields. This is all to say that, whereas reviewing may help the quality of articles overall, it is not a completely objective and value-free process.

Some journals and book publishers complicate things even further by having what they call "blind review." This does not mean that the reviewers are blind—although one might think this on the basis of some of the decisions that they make. Blind reviewing means that traces of the author have been eradicated by not including the author's name on a title page or on the first page or in the header. There are several implications of such an approach. For example, I often recognize who wrote the manuscript I am reviewing because I know the field and who is working in it. This puts me in the awkward position of having to try to pretend, and perhaps even overcompensating by doing so, that I do not know who it is or that I don't know any of his or her other scholarship. On other occasions,

I find myself trying to figure out who the person is. Recently, I was asked to review a manuscript for a journal on whose editorial board I sat. I soon was able to determine that the author was a close friend of mine. I unfortunately had some critical comments to make on it (if nothing else, it shows I was trying my best to give it an objective review). I insisted to the editor that he should ensure that my identity did not get back to the author. A few months later, I was attending a scholarly conference, and the author of the article came over and sat down next to me and soon said, "Thanks for reviewing my article. . . ." Not only was I able to determine who he was, but he could figure out who I was through the kinds of comments that I made. There is no doubt that the reviewing process is far from neutral, completely objective, or even blind.

I think that some journals and book publishers have found this practice of blind review a liability. The result has been that a number of senior scholars have had their works rejected and junior scholars have had theirs accepted. I remember hearing the editor of a journal bragging that his journal had turned down a manuscript submitted by a well-known but unnamed scholar, on the basis of blind review. Why, you might ask, is this a bad thing? Sometimes it clearly is not, when young scholars produce interesting and important work. However, sometimes journals and book publishers and their reviewers fall into the trap of thinking that an article or book has to look a certain way to merit publication—for example, having a certain density of footnotes, a particular structure or shape, and the like—and that meeting such requirements qualifies as scholarship. Often senior scholars, not being in the position of having to worry about such constrictions, will not conform to this supposed norm, and then their article or book gets rejected, even if their mature viewpoint may actually be more worthwhile than the article with every t crossed and i dotted. Besides, publishing journals or monograph series with no senior scholars in them is a way to ensure that fewer people will read them, simply because of the lack of articles by significant contributors to the field in question. This is probably a sad, but understandably true, commentary on both the contributors and the readers.

Some journal editors believe that having up to three (or more?) anonymous reviewers of a manuscript ensures that only the best articles are accepted. I once received an opinion back on a manuscript I had written that had been sent to two different reviewers—and their opinion was split. One thought that the piece made a significant and decisive contribution and should be published, while the other thought that it was fatally flawed and of little merit. (Did they read the same manuscript, or were they simply two different people?) Does this tell me anything about the article, or only about the reviewers? I fear it says more about the reviewing process than the reviewers (incidentally, the article was published by another journal without significant alteration, and I believe that it has clearly made an important new contribution to the field; I guess one of the reviewers was right—but would we have known which one if I had not pursued publication?). Such procedures are clearly not a guarantee that the process results in better journal articles or books being published. In fact, I know that it does not. A scholar was recently asked to review a manuscript for a publishing company. In his opinion, the potential monograph was very deeply flawed, and he took pains to indicate at length its many shortcomings. When he returned the manuscript with comments, he was told that a second reviewer had reached a similar conclusion. My colleague was quite surprised when the monograph soon appeared in print, substantially the same in its body but with an extended introduction addressing many of the issues that he had raised. Such responses by publishers do not lead me to believe that we have attained the best process for making decisions on articles and book manuscripts. I have worked with publications that have large and extensive review procedures and others with streamlined and trim review procedures, and I am not convinced that one produces better results than the other in terms of the quality of its publications. This is all to say that, as an author, you need not get too hung up with the peer-review system. If you do your homework, and (I would like to think) take to heart the guidelines I present in this book, you should have no trouble getting an article accepted in a peer-reviewed journal and a monograph accepted in a peer-reviewed series.

A number of well-known and well-recognized journals and monograph series are not peer reviewed in the ways outlined above or are only reviewed by the editor or an associate. In these cases, the articles or monographs are simply accepted by the editor or a trusted associate on the basis of their opinion, and do not go through the procedure of being sent out for (blind) review by one of the members of an editorial board. An advantage of such a journal or monograph series is that it can often publish either more frequently or more quickly than one that relies upon a rigid peer-review process. Peer-review boards are often made up of senior scholars in the profession who perform this task gratis as their contribution to and reinvestment in the discipline. Therefore, reviewing of articles and book manuscripts often has to await their timing and schedule. Informally reviewed publications have the freedom of foregoing this process and moving straight to acceptance and publication, especially if the manuscript has been solicited by the editor in the first place. In such editorial circumstances, one can always argue that the editor personally serves as the peer who is doing the reviewing—if the person is an active academic, that may well be true. There are many such journals and series in existence, and many even in our professions do not know the difference between them and those that claim to be more strictly peer-reviewed.

Articles and Their Contribution

Having said all of the above, I recognize that it is articles (and monographs) appearing in recognized peer-reviewed publications (or at least ones that have established equivalent academic reputations, whether formally reviewed or not) that establish our research profiles. For that reason, they should not be ignored. Articles in such journals are the ones that heads of departments and deans like to see on job applications and tenure review and promotion documents. They are the ones that at the end of the day we all feel better about mentioning in the lunchroom. These are the articles that have a focused thesis to argue, show command of the major literature, especially the most recent literature, and make a contribution to thought in the field. These articles can take almost any kind of conceivable shape and size (more on that in chapter 4). Some of these include short and focused treatments of a very narrow point, others a broad and sweeping programmatic essay on a broad topic. Most articles will, in their commonest form, develop their theme in sufficient depth to cover the major constructive and critical points. Not to be overlooked here is the critical review of previous literature, as such an article requires that the author demonstrate a firm grasp of the range of material in a given field. Sometimes these review articles can illustrate or shape the latest trends in research. I will also mention the invited essay for a themed issue of a journal or in response to another scholar's essay or book. These last two types—the critical review and the invited paper—gain the kudos of the refereed journal article, often without going through the same editorial scrutiny.

I have written a number of different types of refereed articles. Some present a new hypothesis in the field, while others summarize the state of research in a field. I have even coauthored several articles, especially where it has allowed me to write with a fellow scholar of complementary abilities. For example, in one instance we wrote on the formal logical structure of a particular argument. My coauthor had expertise in symbolic logic, while I placed the argument within the larger field of discussion. The result was a short but convincing contribution to the field.

An article in a refereed journal—and articles in unrefereed journals, if they are recognized and accepted publications—is worth a factor of one in calculating their relative weight toward establishing one's research profile (see chapter 9). I have noticed through the years that the size or scope of the article is almost immaterial but that the fact that the article has been published is crucial. The assumption seems to be that an article of any size requires a certain amount of critical thought, planning, research, and writing. Even a short article requires a minimum level of commitment that is not mathematically balanced by the increased length of a bigger article.

While on the topic, there are a couple of other tips that I may as well include here regarding the publishing of articles. The first is that short articles often have an advantage over longer articles, because they can be used to fill up the remaining pages in a journal. Most journals publish fascicles of standard length, and an editor may need to fill a few pages to make that issue complete. A short article that has been accepted can jump to the front of the publication line in such a circumstance. A second tip is that journals that pride themselves on being international in character but that publish in the English-speaking world often have an underrepresentation of articles in other languages, such as French and German. If you are able to write (or have help in writing) an article in one of these neglected languages, you not only may have an easier time through the peer-review process but may jump to the front of the line for publication, so that the journal can reach some kind of self-imposed quota. A third tip is that those who represent minority voices in a field should take full advantage of that status when considering publication. Many journals, in an effort to be seen as politically correct, will welcome submission of articles from those who have been underrepresented in the profession in the past.

There are literally thousands and thousands of articles published in journals every year. Each and every journal is filled with them every time it appears. The true test of an article is not simply that it has appeared in a given journal, although there are no doubt bragging rights that go along with publication in certain journals. A gifted professor I know had a major article published. This was a lengthy treatment of the subject, and he put great stock in its significance. He was shocked when it appeared—even after due diligence in proofreading—with two pages reversed. He was horrified at the thought that he would be ridiculed by his peers for having let such an avoidable mistake slip through. I think he was even more distressed, however, that no one else seemed to notice the mistake. The true test of an article is whether it endures in the scholarly consciousness. In other words, the test of an article is found in the quality and endurance of its ideas, its willingness to say something sustainably new, and the role that it plays in influencing and developing subsequent scholarship well into the future. Very few peer reviewers, editors, or even authors know the enduring value of an article when it first appears.

Chapters in Collections of Essays

There are often opportunities to contribute chapters to a collection of essays, edited by you or another scholar (see the section above on Edited Volumes). These chapters that make up a volume of essays may come from a number of different sources, either published or unpublished. These volumes include collections of previously published essays, essays written on a particular topic for the specific book project, conference proceedings, essays written in commemoration of an individual (a *Festschrift*, discussed above), and others. Usually such collections comprise contributions by a variety of scholars, but you as an individual scholar may choose to produce a volume of essays of your own previous work. In terms of contribution to scholarship, any of the types mentioned above can reap benefits for you as a scholar—simply reprinting previously published essays, however, will not add to your research profile, although it might keep your name before the scholarly public. As a result, a number of authors always ensure that a reprinted essay is updated, by either adding to the body of the essay or attaching an appendix that responds to criticism of the original article and covers items raised or published since the article first appeared—in which case only the appendix counts for further academic standing.

The chapters themselves in such collected volumes can cover a wide range of topics and approaches, depending upon the occasion and format of the publication. Chapters in collections of essays are not considered refereed publications in the same way a refereed article is, although the

editor approving the essays for publication is a form of reviewing process. If the editor is a reputable scholar, that process helps to guarantee
the status of the volume. The fact that there is no formal review process,
however, does not mean that there are not many valuable essays that have
appeared as chapters in collections of essays. Many significant scholars in
biblical studies, theology and religion, and the arts and humanities have
contributed to such volumes, and many view these essays as among their
most significant. For example, one of the most widely cited essays that
I have published first appeared in a collection of essays from a conference. On the basis of my experience in editing and publishing, I offered
to work with the conference organizer to get the conference proceedings
published. This worked out so well that it led to a number of similar
conferences and publications of collections of essays. The fact that I was
coeditor of the volume has not in any apparent way detracted from the
recognition given to the essay.

Like the journal article, the chapter appearing in a collection of
essays counts as a single unit in the relative weighting of publications (see
chapter 9). Even if an essay is not published in a formally refereed journal, the amount of research involved in producing a significant chapter is
similar. In many ways, in fact, there is greater academic scope provided
by an essay in a collection than by publication in a journal, as journals
are often bound by a variety of arbitrary restrictions, such as length, that
do not usually apply in the same way to creating a collection of essays. I
would not hesitate to make contributions to collections of essays, and to
go further and get involved in being the editor of such collections. Many
significant chapters in such collections have had a recognizable and lasting impact upon an academic discipline.

Dictionary and Encyclopedia Articles

Dictionary and encyclopedia articles are placed at the bottom of the heap
so far as gaining significant recognition for academic publishing. Nevertheless, they can make a useful contribution both to your research profile
and to your academic field.[17] Dictionary and encyclopedia articles, and
their related types of reference materials, are always in demand to be
written, because every dictionary or encyclopedia that is published needs
to have the basic entries for that particular field. I am occasionally asked
to write essays for such volumes, often on similar topics. I have even been
asked at the last minute to do so, when another author clearly bailed out

on the project. Even though I write a new essay for each one, there is often enough similarity to other essays I have written that I am not writing an unrelated essay each time.

There are some advantages to writing dictionary and encyclopedia articles. For example, they are good for exposing their author to new fields and subjects, by acquainting him or her with these topics through writing an essay. Another advantage is that these projects often pay well (at least better than journal articles and chapters in collections of essays) and usually provide a copy of the dictionary or encyclopedia (at least if it is a single volume). At the beginning of my career, I was looking for an opportunity to contribute to such a project so as to get my name known, and I made an effort to meet the assigning editor for a major dictionary project. I volunteered to write on anything available and was given two or three very small entries—after all, I was totally unknown to him. At the time I agreed to write these several articles, I was given a choice of receiving direct payment for the essays or the opportunity to purchase the entire dictionary set (it was to be in multiple volumes) at reduced price when it was finished. I chose to receive payment, as I needed the money at that point in my career more than I needed the books. As it turned out, I was asked to write nearly forty entries for that dictionary project, virtually all of them focused around a single area that (as now seems obvious) few others wished to write on. I was paid enough so that I could buy the entire dictionary twice over at full price—something that I did not do, however. I probably also became the world's greatest living expert in one of the smallest areas of human knowledge.

The limitations of writing dictionary and encyclopedia articles can sometimes be frustrating. The lengths of the articles are usually preset to maintain balance in the overall shape of the project. This circumscribes the length of the article and is sometimes seen as an unwelcome restriction by some authors. My advice is to take the assignment only if you intend to follow the guidelines. Another limitation is that the articles are designed to represent the current state of opinion on the subject, and hence they offer very little scope for entirely new or creative thinking in the discipline. Some find this a nuisance, especially when the editor returns the dictionary entry for revision to ensure that the consensus of the profession is clearly represented. A final limitation is that many dictionary and encyclopedia articles do not want any footnotes or other forms of references to scholarly sources. Some, but not all, allow a bibliography at the end of the entry, but this is not the same as footnotes or parenthetical citations. The idea behind such an arrangement is that the article is meant to represent the standard opinion, and therefore as a received tradition it does not need to be cited by source.

Dictionary and encyclopedia articles are at the bottom of the league table for relative weighting of scholarly importance. A major, lengthy article, or perhaps a set of a number of articles, might be worth one unit of research work (see chapter 9). However, on account of lack of originality, the encyclopedia or dictionary entry article usually does not merit even this weighting.

Book Reviews

Book reviews are important for a scholar to write for several reasons. One reason is that they give the scholar an opportunity to keep abreast of an academic field, or possibly be introduced to one, by reviewing a book in that field and being forced to respond to it both positively and negatively. A second reason is that the reviewer gets to keep the book in return for reviewing it, and hence build a library of important sources for future reference and research work. A free, critically reviewed book gives free knowledge.

Book reviews can take all shapes and sizes, from the short book notice or book note of one hundred to two hundred words that merely summarizes the gist of the book, to a major essay in response to the volume, to a review article that surveys any number of recent books that have appeared in the field. One of the most important lessons that you as a young scholar can learn from book reviews is to be circumspect, especially at the outset of a reviewing career. It is easy in reviewing a book—whether it is because of the relative ease with which it can be done, the lack of a review system of checks and balances, the situation of a young scholar just returning from the rigors (perceived or otherwise) of doctoral study, or any number of other reasons—for the young academic to be overly hard on the book being scrutinized. You need to be careful, because a reputation for being vindictive in reviews is a difficult one to live down and may well result in one not being asked to review many books thereafter. There is nothing so unnerving for a young upstart reviewer as sitting down for a job interview across the table from the author of the book that he or she has recently trashed in print.

Book reviews carry virtually no relative weight in the hierarchy of values of scholarly publications. A review article of a number of conceptually related books, however, especially if it is treated in a journal as the equivalent of a regular article, can count as one unit (see chapter 9), but only if the reviewer goes beyond merely summarizing the books and critically interacts with them in a constructive way that advances knowledge.

Papers for Conferences and Other Invitations

Papers read at conferences and other venues constitute the last category of academic writing that I will mention. The act of giving a paper itself has relatively little academic weight, but there are still good reasons for doing them. I would recommend that every scholar attempt to give several academic papers a year at various conferences, because of the many possibilities they present. I have noted above how papers written for conferences or similar occasions can often be gathered together into a collection of essays. You may wish to be such an editor. Such a process requires some planning ahead in terms of contacting the contributors in advance and letting them know what the expectation for publication is, providing a style sheet so that authors know how to prepare their manuscript (I suggest using one of the standard styles in your respective profession unless the publisher specifies otherwise), and setting a date for delivery of the manuscript to you as editor of the volume.

Delivering papers at conferences has a number of other clear and distinct scholarly advantages. One of the most obvious is that the conference setting gives a scholar an opportunity to try out an idea that he or she might not be able to present elsewhere. In many of our institutions, we may be one of only a few with interest in a specialized academic area, and perhaps the only true specialist in a focused area of teaching and research. Our colleagues may well be interested in our work and very encouraging of our efforts, but a conference of specialists provides a natural next step for trying out our ideas to see if they are viable. There is nothing like the charged atmosphere of a conference session, when you stand up to give a paper on a topic and notice that the two leading experts in the field are sitting in the second and fifth rows, looking like they have not eaten for a week and are ready to devour you. Knowing that this might happen helps you to be sure that your preparation has covered all of the necessary bases before you step boldly forward and present your ideas.

Another advantage of giving papers is that the writer of the complete conference paper has done most of what is necessary for a publication.

The conference itself might be providing an opportunity for publication either through a volume of conference proceedings or, better, a specially edited volume, or perhaps you want to pursue another means. In any case, *I strongly recommend that the paper to be delivered should be written to publication standards and with publication in mind from the outset.* Finding the footnotes or other references at the time of writing cuts way back on the time required later to reconstruct your mind-set when writing the paper and then locating the lost sources. Sometimes this means that you have to abbreviate the comments you deliver at the conference, as conference sessions often do not provide the needed amount of time to present a significant paper for printed publication. By thinking of every conference paper as a potential publication, and doing the required work up front before the paper is delivered, you have a greater chance of publishing the article. Someone might even approach you at the conference with a publication offer on the basis of having heard the presented paper, or may even invite further papers. These are opportunities not to be missed—what better response than to be able to put a copy of the paper directly into the hands of the editor or publisher?

As your scholarly reputation grows, you will probably receive other opportunities to deliver scholarly papers by invitation. You may be invited to give a paper at a conference organized around a particular theme, or you may be the featured speaker at a given conference. These invitations provide tremendous opportunities both to develop your scholarly reputation and, more importantly, to use the occasion to prepare a manuscript for presentation. I have been invited on several occasions to give a series of lectures on a given topic. One of the recent occasions was a series of three public lectures on a designated topic, with publication of the papers as the anticipated outcome. I prepared the manuscript in advance with publication in mind. It meant that I had to abbreviate the papers while I presented them to fit the time constraints, but the full manuscript was much closer to being ready to send to the publisher when finished.

The conference paper does not have any weight in the hierarchy of academic publishing values. However, if you do it right—that is, by preparing the paper in advance as if it were going to be published—there is a much greater chance of the conference paper becoming a journal article or chapter in a book. Certainly invited papers should be treated in this light.

There are several sets of hierarchies that need to be weighed as you examine these types of publications and attempt to calibrate your own academic publishing career. One of these hierarchies involves the relative values of the publication types. The monograph and, after that, some (but not all!) other types of book are at the top of the heap, followed by the refereed journal article, the substantial unrefereed article and chapter in a collection, and then the dictionary and encyclopedia article. There is a similar hierarchy concerning the venues for publication, which will be addressed further in chapter 4. There is a hierarchy of publishers. In terms of academic research publishing, the devoted academic publishers, including university publishers, carry the most weight. These are followed by the publishers who are either niche publishers or who do a mix of academic and trade books. The same is true of journals, with a number of journals in each discipline having established themselves as the benchmarks in their respective disciplines and demanding publication in them if one wishes to establish a strong research profile.[18] This is not to say that good articles do not appear in other types of journals, because they clearly do. It is just that, within a discipline, certain journals, like other publishers, command the most academic attention.

With this framework in place, we can turn to the mechanics of producing publishable scholarship.

2

📖

BASIC PRINCIPLES OF A PUBLISHABLE MANUSCRIPT

The single most important skill that an aspiring scholar can develop is the ability to write and to write well. There is no substitute for the ability to craft your writing so that it conveys what you wish for it to express, rather than simply being an undisciplined series of words. I still find it amazing how many scholars are genuinely awful writers—even some who have huge academic reputations. I was made acutely aware of this early in my own publishing career when I was coediting a collection of essays by other academics. This collection drew together papers by a number of well-known scholars. As we began to receive the essays, I was struck by how badly some of them read. They required a lot of work to be brought up to a reasonable standard. I realized then that many of these authors had been greatly helped by their editors, such as me and my coeditors. The truth be told, if it had been up to us as editors alone, we would have returned or even rejected some of the essays because they were so poorly written. But, because we wanted the prestige of their names in the volume, we did the dirty work of revising their poor prose.[1]

I studied English quite a bit in high school, and then earned B.A. and M.A. degrees in English literature, so I read a lot of great writing and had to write a lot myself as part of my programs of study. I learned to write quickly and efficiently, however, when I was the editor of my undergraduate college newspaper. There were more days than I would like to recount when the deadline for submission of articles had come and one of my reporters had failed to produce a promised or anticipated article. So I had to sit down at the keyboard of my basic electric typewriter—but without automatic correction—and hammer out enough copy to fill the week's newspaper. Not only because of the lack of auto-correction, but because of the impending deadline (to say nothing of the fact that the typewriter had an electrical short in it so that a number of letters had a tendency to repeat), I learned how to write the first draft as the last draft of the articles I needed. I have been able to benefit from this ability many times since (I know what you might be thinking, did I hammer out this book in a single draft? No, I have edited the manuscript several times). Nevertheless, there were still a number of times along the way when I had to relearn my writing craft. When I was in graduate school, I will never forget the day I received back my first paper from one of my professors. As we went through the paper together, he pointed out numerous places where my writing was not idiomatic, or I used the wrong preposition, or I mixed metaphors. This forced me to rethink my entire writing process, so that when I wrote I weighed each word, each clause, each sentence, and each paragraph. This ability to scrutinize every construction came in handy in another course in my master's degree. The professor said that he would only read the entire final paper for those students who convinced him to do so on the basis of the first two pages of their paper. Needless to say, I worked incredibly hard to make those two pages as close to word- and concept-perfect as I could. I needed to include enough material in the two pages to entice the professor to want to read further, and do so in a way that came as close to stylistic perfection as I could (in answer to your question, I was one of three whose entire papers he read, out of a group of seventeen).

As a result of paying attention to writing through the years, I have discovered a number of techniques that I have had occasion to use with students and colleagues. I have taught English composition and literature—my first teaching job was as an English composition instructor—and these have come in handy both for my own writing and for my development of the writing of others. That does not mean that I still do not need to pay attention to my own writing style—I do. Under the pressure of writing a piece that is overdue, I too fall into the traps of poor word choice, clumsy clauses, or awful sentences.

In this chapter, I wish to discuss basic principles of creating a publishable manuscript, so that authors of any ability can improve their writing so as to create a piece worthy of being accepted by a publisher. I then address how to create publishable manuscripts for both the scholarly article and the monograph. This process includes (1) rethinking the writing process, (2) constructing a publishable academic paper, and (3) constructing a publishable academic book.

Rethinking the Writing Process

This may seem very basic, but rethinking the writing process is still a very important place to begin. I have three basic suggestions that I think—in fact, I know—can improve anyone's writing.

The first is to subject your writing to critical scrutiny. This means that you must learn to critically read your own writing and be willing to have someone else read it who will be completely honest with you.[2] I will talk further about this in the final chapter, but I think that getting someone else to read your writing is very valuable. In any case, whether you read it yourself or you have someone else read it, the person reading must be willing and able to be completely honest regarding the writing. The human capacity for self-deception is probably only exceeded by the capacity for deception of others, and writing is subject to both such deceptions.

Writing is a lot like giving birth to a baby, or so my college creative writing professor once said. The parent of a new child honestly thinks that their baby is the most beautiful and adorable thing ever brought into this world, and will not stand for anyone saying otherwise. If you don't believe this is true, next time you see a parent strolling with a baby, go up to the parent and tell them how ugly or odd-looking their child is. You had better be prepared to defend yourself! Writing is a lot like that. When you write something, there is an investment of emotional, intellectual, and creative energy that makes it difficult to be honest and self-critical about the writing. One of the best cures for this is to set the writing aside for a period of time and return to it later. I have found that often only a couple of days' hiatus is necessary. A week is probably even better. The passage of time helps to sever the parental bond with our writing so that we can take a look at it with more self-critical and honest eyes. This honesty is invaluable for a good evaluation of the writing.

Sometimes it is simply too hard to arrive at a reasonable opinion of our own writing, and it is necessary to get the opinion of someone else. Bringing someone in to our writing process can potentially be a very precarious situation. We run the risk of exposing ourselves to another who may not be as pleased with our prose as we are. Showing your writing to someone else is a lot like asking someone for their honest opinion of whether your baby is beautiful. Both sides need to be careful that they do not say too much or too little, not erring on the side of being too honest or offering too little truth. Showing your writing to another requires that the person you ask be allowed to comment critically on the writing. As a writer, you need to be able to expose your personal creative work to the potential criticism of others. Otherwise the entire process only produces misperceptions. There is no benefit in showing writing to a person who will simply tell you what you want to hear: that the writing is the greatest thing since Dickens. The person is being dishonest and setting you up for an even greater disappointment when the editor of the journal or monograph series responds negatively, perhaps even stating that whatever good ideas there are in the piece are lost in the midst of inadequate prose. The secret to being a good reader of others' writing is to be honest and critical, but kind.

The second suggestion concerns what you should look for in evaluating writing. This book is not the place to give a lesson in English composition. I will assume that you know the basics of how to write—including the technical dimensions of writing English prose; the ways in which suitable footnotes are created; and how an argument is created, organized, and pursued. These are givens (although I have seen much evidence to the contrary). However, each one of them needs to be scrutinized in the course of evaluating your writing. A secret that I have realized is that the human brain is an incredible organ, and it will often indicate the places where remedial work is needed. As I read through my own work or the work of others—assuming that all of the above basic items have been taken care of—I often notice where I am stopped by the writing and forced to reread a sentence or even a paragraph. At these places, I stumble and need to take a closer look at the potential problem. Sometimes it may be a matter as simple as poor word choice or improper punctuation. These are relatively easy to fix so that the reading can go on unhindered. Some of the time, however, the problems are more serious. They may include the failure of the argument to proceed logically from step to step. One step in the argument may be missing, or there may be too many assumptions that are not evident or articulated. These kinds of problems can often be solved by rewriting a very short passage or section of the manuscript. There are some problems, however, that are of potential catastrophic consequence. These occur when vital portions of the argument are skipped or, even worse, distorted or misinterpreted, so that the consequences that follow are not logically legitimate. These kinds of errors—we hope that they are few—require far more serious help to address. They often require substantial writing of a new or different paragraph, or even an entire section of an essay or chapter.

The third suggestion is a virtually certain means for improving one's writing. I found that, whether teaching English composition or working with scholarly colleagues, there was often a basic inability to write consistently fluent and coherent English prose. I remember when one of the most intelligent and certainly one of the most ambitious students I ever had admitted to me that he could not write very well. I unfortunately knew this to be the case from having read his writing. It was not that there were many obvious grammatical mistakes, but the writing was not tight, did not cohere, and often slipped into a colloquial style that just was not pitched correctly for academic prose. I told him that if he sincerely wanted to learn how to write he would need to do the following, and that it would guarantee his success as a writer (he did it, and it did!). I believe that if a writer undertakes to do this, similar results are a possibility.

The best means that I know of improving your writing involves the following straightforward process. Sit down with an essay that you have written and rewrite it in the following way. Begin with the first sentence, and rewrite that sentence ten different ways using different words. Move to the next sentence and do the same. Then move to the third sentence and rewrite it, and do this all the way through the essay. This sounds excessive—and perhaps it is—but it turns the tables on the writing process. One of the major difficulties for writers is to control their language, rather than having the language control them. This method ensures that you control your writing. Ten different ways of writing and rewriting a sentence means that you must consider and make a number of different lexicographical and syntactical choices that had not been previously tried. When you choose one over the other—or in some rare cases, realize that a satisfactory sentence has not yet been found and continue rewriting until it is—you know why that particular sentence works and the others do not. You then have a more intimate and informed knowledge of the various ways in which a given thought may be expressed and nuanced, and have consciously chosen the one that is most appropriate in the context.

I would suggest that when you try this technique you do it with pen and paper, and not simply on the computer. Writing and rewriting the examples may work on the computer, but for most writers there is not the intimacy of tactile connection with the writing process that occurs when you actually use a pen and paper. In fact, at least at the early stages, I believe that most authors are much better in writing, editing, and proofreading with pen and paper rather than on-screen. I know of many scholars who, because they did not learn the process of writing and editing their writing with pen and paper, never developed later in their careers as the writers and editors they might have, since they remained glued to the computer screen and keyboard. I know that the above writing technique works, because I have used it myself on many occasions to refine my own writing, and because I have seen it work to improve the writing of students and colleagues. One successful example is the student mentioned above who published the essay he had written while a junior in college.

There are a number of works available on the market designed to help scholars and others improve their writing. Some of them are probably very useful—although none of them will be as helpful as they might be unless you make a serious effort to put into practice the advice that is given.[3]

Constructing a Publishable Academic Paper

Even if you have mastered the fundamentals of writing, there is still the question of how you go about constructing a publishable journal article. One of the obvious potential sources for publishable academic papers is papers written while you were a graduate student. After all, the demand of writing a paper for a graduate seminar or class requires the kind of research, critical thinking, and presentation of arguments that would seem to be ready-made for publication in an academic journal or collection of essays. I agree. The first journal article I published was a revised version of a paper written for an advanced seminar at the master's level, and the first essay I published in a collection of essays was a revised form of a paper prepared for another master's-level course.

There is no doubt that the research done at the graduate level can be the basis for a publishable academic paper, but there are also a number of other factors to keep in mind: the structure, organization, documentation, and conclusion. Each of these needs to be treated individually.

The first major factor in constructing a publishable journal article is to learn the structure of an academic journal article. Nowhere that I know of is this form taught, even though the standard form of a term paper written for a class assignment is not the form usually demanded by scholarly academic publishing. The standard term-paper format—even in graduate programs—often follows what is sometimes called the funnel structure.[4] Think of a funnel, a tube that runs down from the funnel, and an inverted funnel at the other end. This is one of the major ways that students are taught to construct essays, and this format for constructing an essay travels with them throughout their academic career. I know, because I was taught this way and I myself taught this form of essay writing in numerous college English writing courses. The funnel structure says that the author should start broad in the introduction, and then narrow down to a particular thesis statement. That thesis statement is then developed throughout the essay, until the essay concludes by placing the essay once again within a broad context. For all the virtues of this essay structure, use of it is unlikely to ensure that the essay is published in an academic journal.

The structure of the academic article is probably the single most important factor—besides having something significant to say—in guaranteeing its publishing success. The problem is that there is no one set structure. Nevertheless, rather than the funnel-tube-funnel structure of so many essays, I suggest that most well-crafted academic articles follow a simple cylinder structure, with a thesis statement at or near the beginning of the essay and each substantial point following one after the other. In any case, whatever shape the final essay takes, I recommend that you begin with a very clear focus for your essay and that your thesis statement appear very close to the front of the essay, at or near the top of the cylinder.

As we have already noted, it is important to differentiate between the subject or topic of an essay and the thesis that you wish to argue. The subject is what the essay is broadly about. The subject or topic of an essay might be the theology of Karl Barth, open theism, the Ottoman Empire, Britain in World War II, Slavic nationalism in the late nineteenth century, or whatever. The thesis statement is what you, as an author, wish to say about the subject. The thesis of an essay might be that Karl Barth was not a neo-orthodox theologian but the first postmodern theologian, that the Ottoman Empire collapsed because of the incompatibility of its political system with the spread of rising nationalism, or that Britain's delay in entering World War II meant that it had to fight from a defensive posture that jeopardized the results and its role in the postwar era.[5] This thesis statement needs to be (1) significant enough to warrant the essay and the arguments and evidence that you are going to marshal; (2) concise enough to be developable and memorable within the space of a single essay; (3) focused enough to command the attention of your readers; and (4) expandable enough to provide the basic development, structure, or support of the essay. Failure in any of the areas can imperil the success of the essay. I like to begin the writing process by explicitly stating what my thesis is going to be and then working that statement over until I believe that it captures what I want to say and fulfills the four criteria just mentioned. This often involves a number of rewrites of the statement (but if you are experienced with the method introduced above, this should pose no problem). I often find that the structure of this thesis statement will contain several subpoints that will then determine the shape of the essay itself. I then have this thesis statement prominent at the top of the page or the top of the essay, or in some readily perceivable place, because it needs to determine whether anything that I consider writing is or is not finally included in the essay. If a statement or point does not have a clear relationship to the thesis statement, such as offering proof, development, possible objection, or the like, then I have to ask whether that statement—as brilliantly stated as it may be and as difficult to delete as it may seem—belongs in the essay, or whether it is an extraneous statement that detracts from the impact that I am trying to make.

The second major element of your academic paper is the organization itself. Here there is a fair bit of flexibility that is allowed, depending on a number of factors. Some of these factors include the nature of the essay, such as whether it is a review of scholarship or something far more focused, whether there has been much previous discussion of the topic in the secondary literature, or whether this is an idea with little precedent. Related to the organization is the length of the essay. A shorter essay will tend to have a much more compact and streamlined organization than a longer essay, as a shorter essay will likely be even more closely focused on a limited thesis. Another factor is the type of argumentation that is being used in the individual paragraphs and in the paper itself. There are a number of standard ways of organizing both individual paragraphs and, sometimes, the entire paper. It is wise to think deliberately about the organizational plan of each paragraph, as well as the overall shape of the paper, and to use suitable forms of argumentation. These types of organization include definition, description, comparison and contrast, example, classification and division, cause and effect, and even narration.[6] In all cases, the organization of your essay needs to ensure that the structure and organization chosen are appropriate and suitable to the length, the type of essay, and the argumentative style that is being used. The organization needs to be logical at every point, whether the arguments are constructive or deconstructive in nature.[7] The organization needs to be tight and focused.

One of the keys to any writing, including both papers and longer works, is the need for appropriate signposts that indicate to the reader where he or she is in the course of reading through the essay.[8] Even experienced authors often fail to provide the necessary signposts to guide readers from start to finish. Writers often think that because they (think they) know where they are in the development of a particular argument, their readers instinctively know as well. This is simply not so. As the old adage for a sermon or speech goes, you need to tell them what you are going to do, do it, and then tell them what you have done. I would add further that, in the course of your doing it, you need to tell your reader what you are doing as well. Signposts can consist of any number of different linguistic devices. Sometimes signposts consist of suitable transition statements between major divisions or paragraphs. These are crucial for letting the reader know that an important point is being reached in the essay, by bringing one unit to a close and then introducing a new one. At other times, you may need to use not only a simple statement as a signpost but a set of sentences or even an entire paragraph. Signposts also consist of suitable headings and subheadings to mark the various units within an essay or a chapter. No matter what signposts are used, even these are not a substitute for discursive writing that lays out clearly where the reader is in the argument. It may seem at times that so many signposts are redundant, because they seem to mark everything out so clearly as to insult the reader. In my experience, I have rarely if ever (in fact, as I think about it, never) seen a piece of serious writing that has too many signposts in it, but I have read plenty of academic papers, chapters in books, and even entire monograph manuscripts that were woefully lacunate in signposts.

The third factor is the required amount of documentation and secondary literature. In a subsequent chapter, I will refer to the various recognized methods of documentation. Here I wish simply to say that the documentation needs to be suitable and appropriate, both in quantity and type, for the kind of paper or chapter or even book that you are writing. Again, different types of essays have different styles of documentation. As discussed in chapter 1 above, a dictionary article may have no explicit secondary references but merely be a compendium of received tradition on a subject. However, most scholarly writing requires some form of documentation. Those essays that are confined to using a social-scientific method may limit the quantity and type of documentation as well, especially if they do not allow the use of footnotes or, more particularly, of content footnotes. Even those essays that use the traditional notational method, however, have some restrictions on the amount of documentation. Typical of many doctoral dissertations is documentation ad nauseum, to the point where every author who ever lived, breathed, or wrote a comment on a particular point is cited in a footnote, even if the cited scholar is entirely derivative and adds nothing to the discussion. Such, unfortunately, is the degraded state of some doctoral research, where the creation of lengthy footnotes is confused with genuine scholarship. Such footnoting is not only unnecessary but inappropriate for most scholarly writing. Even so, there is a wide range of documentation levels, from a single reference to a source of a quotation, to a brief listing of the key people who have held to a particular position, to a more detailed discussion of the development of the particular point being made. The nature of the publication can give you guidance here regarding the level of documentation.

One of the common mistakes that scholars fall into is thinking that the one style of footnoting that they are most comfortable with or that they have developed over the years is the only type of footnoting, and then using it in every publication that they compose. This descends to the point of some scholars simply transporting—through the wonders of cutting and pasting on their computers—entire lengthy footnotes from one article or chapter to another (and introducing all sorts of inconsistencies of style and first and subsequent references along the way). I recommend instead that you find the type of footnoting appropriate to the particular journal or monograph series or volume and use that type of footnoting. I, for example, have written some papers that are very sparse in documentation because the publication demanded that level of reference, and others that are heavily footnoted. I once consciously wrote an entire book that could be read at two levels—one as a scholarly treatment of a particular well-known academic topic, and the other as a thorough bibliographical commentary presented in the style of the major school of thought that had dominated treatment of the subject.

Related to the type of documentation is the use of foreign literature. In some subjects this is not an issue, such as particular English writers or composers or historical figures for whom there has been little discussion outside of the English-speaking world. In such instances, there is no need to be concerned (once you have checked to be sure) with the foreign-language secondary literature. There are a number of subjects, however, where it is expected that you cite the best and latest foreign-language sec-

ondary literature. The ability to use these sources where they are available often distinguishes good scholarship from mediocre or even poor
scholarship. There is a tendency by some to access this literature through
the work of other scholars, or to cite only literature that has already
passed into the received tradition of a discipline. Relying upon such a
method runs the risks of not appreciating the full argument that you are
making, as you are dependent upon the work of others to summarize and
evaluate it accurately, or of perhaps missing out on important discussion
that may influence the shape of your argument. Most good journals will
expect the citation of the most recent and significant scholarly literature,
no matter what language it appears in.

   The final factor to consider briefly is the conclusion. Having explicitly stated the thesis of the paper, organized it suitably for the topic and
style of presentation, and documented the argument appropriately, at some
point you will (it is hoped!) bring the essay to a close. Instead of using
the inverted funnel mentioned above, a scholarly essay such as this may
need nothing more than a simple restatement (remember the signposts)
of what has been argued and proved in the essay. On some occasions
it may be appropriate for you to expand the conclusion by stating what
the next steps of investigation may be. Certainly one rarely needs to tie the
essay into the world, the universe, and everything. These will take care
of themselves.

Constructing a Publishable Academic Book

A great mystery often surrounds the writing of a book or monograph.
After all, a monograph is long and involves many chapters and the handling of many sources. Putting all of these elements together into a single, cohesive whole is too much, for some people, even to contemplate.
No doubt publishers contribute to some of this confusion by the variety
of books they publish. There is no typical size for a scholarly monograph,
but many publishers get somewhere around 400 words per page, and often
their books are around 250 pages. This means around 100,000 words in
total, give or take a few thousand words for the preliminary pages at
the beginning and the pages of indexes at the end. As you can see, it is
not surprising that many Ph.D. theses are not quite up to the length of
a standard monograph (it seems to be a trend to have dissertations of
around 80,000 words these days). This simply adds to the anxiety. After
all, you may think that it took several years of concerted effort to write

an acceptable thesis of 80,000 words, and now I'm telling you that it needs to be even longer. Then, when you consider that I also said above that you probably need to cut out a lot of the redundant and ridiculously long footnotes, you are gasping at the thought of producing more words.

Relax. In many ways, a monograph is simply a series of individual essays, joined tightly together by a strong and coherent thesis statement. In chapter 1 above, we discussed some of the various types of books that you might write. All of them consist of a series of chapters, some of which may have existed previously, but all of which are joined together into a coherent whole. In other words, much of what we have discussed in the section directly above regarding a publishable journal article is directly applicable to the publishable book—except that it is longer and involves several of the same thing, that is, several of the individual essays mentioned above.

The publishable monograph or book—at least as much as, if not more so than, the article—demands a strong thesis statement. This thesis statement needs to be significant enough, sustainable enough, and important enough not just for an article but to sustain the argumentative weight of an entire monograph. Monographs have a little more latitude than an article in how they are introduced—they have things like prefaces, forewords, and the like—but the introduction or the first chapter should begin strongly with a clear and forceful presentation of the thesis statement, and at least a preliminary development of how the argument will unfold. As with the thesis statement of an article, the thesis of a monograph may well set the agenda for the entire book, by establishing the major parts or even chapters of the entire work. This opening must capture the attention of the reader. No doubt more monographs could stand to begin with something interesting that draws the reader into the book. Although it is not always possible, I like to think that the same criteria for writing an interesting nonscholarly book apply to writing the scholarly monograph. It should be interesting and hold readers' attention so that they want to read more. It is not absolutely essential to a good monograph to bore the reader to tears, and there is more than a little merit in creating interest and anticipation in the subject.

Similarly, the organization of the monograph needs to be appropriate, logical, and tightly constructed in at least two major ways. The first is in terms of the scope and shape of the entire monograph. There is an overall structure that needs to hold all of the individual chapters together. The second is in terms of the individual chapters. These chapters may vary according to how a given chapter functions within the entire monograph. I have found that books with widely varying types of organization and length of their individual chapters find it more difficult to construct a coherent overall argument for the work. There is something to be said for balancing the major parts of the book. The level and type of documentation for a book must also be taken into account. It is not uncommon to find that the kind and level of documentation used in an article are simply too much for a monograph, although that is not always the case. You need to decide the level and type of documentation according to the requirements of the subject and the particular publisher.

The conclusion is one of the most neglected parts of a monograph. In fact, it is not uncommon to find a book without a conclusion. This is reasonable if the introduction has strongly introduced the topic and each individual chapter has a suitable conclusion that ties the chapter into the argument as a whole (those signposts again). However, often a book needs a concluding chapter simply to tie all of the threads together in one place. Such a chapter need not be particularly long but must be substantial enough to perform the task of indicating to the reader what the current state of play is as a result of this particular volume. There is also the opportunity, if appropriate, to suggest further areas of research. (In this sense, the conclusion of a book can resemble the inverted funnel.) One distracting flaw of the conclusions of some monographs, however, is the introduction of entirely new topics of discussion. These new hares are set running, as if a new book has suddenly begun. I find that, as a result, I am often left unsatisfied with the volume. If the new topics were that important, they should have been discussed in the body of the book. If they were not, then they should not have been included in the volume at all.

This chapter has provided basic knowledge regarding the writing process. For some young scholars this may seem remedial, but I have found that there are even experienced writers who need some retuning of their writing abilities. For those of you new to academic publishing, you may well need to work on developing your writing abilities. Being able to write clearly and well—though many experienced scholars have not actually gained this facility—is invaluable for anyone who wishes to make an enduring and lasting contribution to scholarship. If you have not developed this ability at this stage, now is the time to master it. Even experienced scholars may also benefit from rethinking the process of writing an academic article, chapter, or monograph. The construction of a compelling and attractive journal article or monograph does not occur by accident but is the result of planning and hard work dedicated to mastering what is required by the subject and by issues of suitable presentation.

3

Always Writing for Publication

The first two chapters were concerned with some of the technical issues concerning writing for academic publication. These include the various types of publications and how they are relatively weighted according to prestige and contribution to the field, and the mechanics of putting together a publishable article or monograph. In a subsequent chapter, I will deal more specifically with the actual mechanics of submitting article and book manuscripts to publishers (chapter 5). In this chapter, I shift the focus from technical definitions and procedures to creation of a life orientation to publishing—that is, a mind-set of always writing for publication.

Throughout our schooling in North America, we have teachers who set our assignments for us, and who tell us when these assignments are due and what the penalties are for failing to accomplish these tasks on time. Many of you who are reading and using this book, like me, are now sitting on the other side of the teacher's desk, so to speak, and we are now making similar demands of our students. Few graduate schools make a concerted effort to teach their students how to become self-motivated so that they do not need deadlines imposed by others and instead become self-activated contributing and publishing scholars in their fields (some even discourage their doing this, which I have noted above in the introduction). Graduate schools often do an excellent job of training their students in the subject matter and may even have provided opportunities for students to gain valuable teaching experience. Few of the programs, however, build into their training how to be transformed from student to scholar in the sense of one who is regularly and actively engaged in publishing and making a contribution through scholarship.

I am not sure why this is the case, but I can imagine all sorts of possible reasons. Some of these institutions may still believe in the old-fashioned pedagogical method of teaching by mute example. That is, the students see the professors doing scholarship and supposedly learn by this unspoken example. But do the students really ever see this take place? They may see their professors teaching in the classroom, examining students, or even possibly socializing with them, but how many of the professors have their students watching them do research for an article, write it at their desk, revise it at home, and send it off for publication? Very few that I know of. Other institutions perhaps do not think that this is a valuable skill to teach their students, as most of them will not end up as scholarly contributors to the discipline but as teachers in predominantly teaching environments. There is probably some truth to the notion that only 20 percent of the scholars in a profession produce about 80 percent of the significant published scholarship. I would have thought that most graduate schools would want their students to aspire to more than mediocrity, however. There is still the problem of how the 20 percent learn when there is no instruction. The reality is that students, even at the undergraduate level, apparently get more interested in their discipline if they are exposed to scholarship by their teachers. I believe that students appreciate the opportunity to work alongside and under the direction of a scholar who is active in academic discussion, far more than simply hearing from someone who stands on the sidelines and comments on what others are doing. A last possible explanation for the lack of instruction is that perhaps there are some scholars who are just downright afraid of their ambitious graduate students. As a result, these scholars may (delusionally) say to themselves that they had it tough when they were students and got no guidance in how to publish, so they are not about to provide such help for their students—after all, if these students are as bright as they think they are, they will figure it out. Well, with this book, I hope that you can figure it out more easily.

This chapter addresses the issue of how to establish a continuing scholarly publishing lifestyle. Two major factors considered here are (1) time management and discipline, and (2) making all your work count.

Time Management and Discipline

One of the most important lessons to learn in order to develop a publishing lifestyle is that you will have to take personal responsibility for it.

When you were a student, the professor set the assignments and their deadlines—these deadlines all become self-imposed when you become a teacher/scholar yourself. I realize that there are important checkpoints such as tenure review or promotion—the phrase "publish or perish" comes to mind, so I realize that these are very real pressures and incentives—but how you acquire the necessary publications to pass through these reviews is left up to you. Plenty of things keep any scholar busy year round, but things to keep a junior scholar busy are especially plentiful. There are all of the new course preparations, sometimes as many as three or four in a given year. New faculty members want to be sure to show that they are fully prepared, know their material, and can delve into new areas. There are also the pressures of teaching itself, especially in this highly competitive MTV environment, in which students' attention spans seem to be the length of a contemporary music video, or the space between commercials on a television show. And these students demand the same kinds of entertaining graphics that they see on television, in movies, or in their computer games. There are also the various administrative responsibilities that a new faculty member is often saddled with. These are often related to student matters, and of course we all want to be popular with our students and be seen to be carrying our full load in the department.

At the end of the day or week or term, there is very little time for scholarship. Few publishers are going to write to a junior scholar and, acting as a surrogate teacher or parent, say that your manuscript is due to them on a particular day, or you will be penalized—because there is no real tangible penalty (the exception is the contract for the long-overdue book, which publishers may cancel). In some ways, I believe that research or study leaves can be one of the worst things with which to entice academics, because they encourage the notion that one can let scholarship slide during the course of the regular year but make up for it during the research leave. I wish scholarship were turned on and off as easily as a water tap, but it simply is not the case. To be a contributing scholar, you must manage all your time, including—or especially—the time available during the academic year.

One of the most important disciplines that you as a new faculty member can and should cultivate—and a junior- or senior-level faculty member should reinstigate if he or she has not already—is that of time management so that scholarship has a place in your regular routine. There is no surrogate teacher standing over you with the kind of control and influence of a graduate professor. The motivation for creating the life of a publishing scholar will, for the most part, need to be self-generated and self-motivated. With all of the responsibilities noted above, you will have to carve time out of an already full day—perhaps early in the morning or late at night after the family has gone to bed. An unwritten paper does not make demands on your time the way that other things and people do—to write that paper requires the kind of discipline that I am suggesting needs to be made a part of your regular routine. Some find that they need uninterrupted blocks of time to do scholarship, while others can work in smaller units of time. Some work early, and others late. Most need to set aside at least some time each day for scholarship. Whatever the case, these portions of time devoted to scholarship need to be a part of your regular routine.

Having said that, I believe that there are also a few shortcuts that can be taken to help create a publishing lifestyle while doing the things that are a regular part of an academic's professorial life. Some of these are described in the next section.

Making All Work Count

One of the taboos of many academic institutions is that students cannot submit the same work twice for a grade. Thankfully there is not a similar stricture on the work of scholars. As a result, there are a number of kinds of work that are routinely done in the course of an academic's life that can be translated into publishable pieces and help to create a publishing lifestyle out of activities that academics are already involved in. Besides the article or book written from scratch, here are some of these projects, and how to think about them.

Doctoral Dissertation

I am still shocked at how many doctoral dissertations are never published, because—if at all possible—the dissertation should be a scholar's first published book. Perhaps the failure to publish is because many of the dissertations are written on uninspired or trivial subjects and do not genuinely deserve more attention. I think that some of the blame for this must be laid at the feet of doctoral supervisors who fail on two counts: to encourage the right kinds of subjects and to supervise the right kinds of dissertations.[1] These supervisory shortcomings do not necessarily mean that a dissertation cannot or should not be published, as I will make clear.

When selecting a doctoral dissertation topic, the student should be encouraged to select a topic that is "publishable, either in whole or in part" (as some of the regulations for granting doctoral degrees in European universities state). This means that one should be able to turn the dissertation into a series of significant articles or into an entire monograph. A way to ensure that this becomes the case, in my experience, is to encourage doctoral students to find research topics that fulfill at least two criteria (besides of course the necessary requisites of any doctoral research, including originality, a clear thesis, documentation, etc.). The first requirement is that the student handle one of the recognized areas of the discipline. This is not usually hard to do, but it is surprising what some students come up with and their supervisors sometimes allow. Some students wish to explore the entire discipline, while others want to invent their own new discipline, while still others are interested in exploring only the most obscure backwater. Apart from the related issues of developing appropriate teaching areas and encouraging employability, those who address the recognized areas of the discipline, I believe, are in a better position to publish their work, because there is already a recognized market and set of academic conversation partners. The second criterion is that the student should take an orientation to the body of material that distinguishes their work from that of everyone else who works on the same body of material. This is perhaps easier said than done, but is an invitation for students to develop cutting-edge methods in their discipline and then apply them in ways that genuinely push the discipline forward. This combination of material and approach is ready-made for publishing success.

The second major factor to consider in writing a doctoral dissertation is to write it from the start as a good book. As one of my mentors once wisely said, no doctoral dissertation ever failed because it was written as too good a book (if it does fail, there may be something wrong with the educational institution). We are trained to think that there are certain conventions that simply must be found in a satisfactory doctoral dissertation. Some of these include the tedious and lengthy survey of previous research; the cumbersome and stilted section that defines the problem and states the method to be used; and the lengthy, inclusive, and stultifying footnotes, to name some that I dislike the most. Each one of these can be rethought from the start so that nothing essential is lost while creating a dissertation that has the appeal of a novel—or at least a good monograph.

When as an editor I work with authors on revising their manuscripts from dissertations into books, one of the things that I often challenge them to consider is what it is that grabs their interest when they pick up a book to read. A good book has to capture our interest in the first few pages or we probably won't continue to read it. The same is true with a dissertation. If the dissertation begins with the statement of purpose and method and then goes into a lengthy survey of research, fully annotated with massive footnotes referring to everyone who ever thought of the topic, there is a good chance that the reader will abandon the work before getting very far—certainly an editor might. I know from my experience as an editor that editors often make up their minds on a manuscript on the basis of reading less than the first fifty pages—truth be told, it is probably the first ten to twenty pages. If they read the rest of the manu-script, it is usually only to confirm their earlier opinion. Only one who is compelled to read such a work will continue, and there are few of these apart from the members of a doctoral committee (and there is sometimes even a question whether they have bothered to read all the way through).

I would suggest that you view the writing of the dissertation as you would the writing of a novel. The opening should create an interest in the topic, by stating the problem in an appealing and enticing way. This should lead to the major discussion of the arguments, each one presented in as intriguing a way as is justifiable. What is the harm of thinking of the process of intellectual discovery in terms reminiscent of a mystery, with each chapter tantalizingly inviting the reader to plunge further into the subject? Remember, as with an interesting book, a dissertation is in many ways just a tightly connected series of individual chapters. Each one provides an opportunity to reignite the curiosity of the reader. Such problematic elements as the survey of research can be handled in a variety of ways also. It is sometimes suitable to break up such a discussion and intersperse it throughout the dissertation, with portions in each chapter as relevant. Or perhaps the survey of research would make an excellent appendix at the end, to which reference is made in the body of the work. Footnotes can be pared down and still make it clear that the dissertation's writer has a handle on all of the pertinent and important literature in the field and can sift it accordingly.

With these guidelines firmly in mind, you can think of the doctoral dissertation as your first book. After all, there is probably no other period of time in a scholar's life when you have such a concentrated time for sustained research as during doctoral study. Once having completed the rigors, as an author you should take full advantage of the work that has been produced, rather than simply shoving it aside and starting over on something else that you may have preferred to write on. I would encourage you who wrote master's theses to consider reexamining this research as the source of possible publications as well. As I mentioned before, my master's thesis became the inspiration (and partial content) for an entire technical monograph. The bulk of the thesis became the substance of perhaps one-quarter of the monograph, and I added new material for the other three-fourths and it created a nice, tidy monograph on a highly specialized topic.

Papers Delivered at Conferences

As discussed in chapter 1, conferences provide a wonderful opportunity for the writing of papers that can lead to publication. I wish to expand on some of my previous comments here.

One of the ways that junior faculty members make sure that their senior colleagues take note of them is to volunteer for various departmental responsibilities. A ready-made opportunity is to be found in volunteering to organize a conference. I have organized or coorganized at least fifteen conferences in the last fifteen or so years, as I mentioned, and I have, as a result, published at least a dozen papers and edited or coedited nearly as many conference volumes as a result. My first edited volume was by far the most difficult because of my inexperience, but they got progressively easier as I learned what I needed to do, what could be done by the contributors to the volume, what could be done by others (and now, what could be done by my junior colleagues), and what could be done by institutional support staff. Over a number of years, with regular conference events taking place, there are a number of scholars I can count on who are willing to participate in them and deliver excellent publishable papers, and there are other scholars who are interested in being asked to attend. The organizing of such a conference provides a number of publishing opportunities. These include the delivery of a paper and subsequent publication, and the editing of the volume of essays. I would try to ensure that, if I were to organize such a conference, I at least got the opportunity to present and publish one of the papers, if not edit the resulting volume as well.

There are a couple of important points to remember when preparing a paper to deliver at a conference, whether or not you are organizing the conference or editing the conference proceedings. When I prepare a paper for a conference—I have delivered over 180 of them—I try to prepare a paper that is as close to a final draft for publication purposes as I can. This does not always work out as well as I would like, due to general busyness, but it is the ideal that I seek and usually achieve. Note that above I said I prepare a draft for publication purposes, not necessarily geared to the time slot allocated at the conference. There is often a difference in the requirements for a paper prepared for oral presentation and one readied for written publication. Conferences are organized differently, and the time slots allocated for papers vary greatly. Some current conference formats don't even allow the participants to deliver the paper, but only to introduce it and then to answer questions. Sometimes only twenty minutes are allocated for a paper, while at the other extreme one may have up to a full hour. Sometimes it is better to read the paper, but other times it is better to paraphrase and summarize while speaking to PowerPoint slides, while at still other times it is better to combine the two. You can see that the requirements for presenting a paper in such circumstances can vary greatly.

The technical requirements for a published academic paper do not vary that significantly. There are fairly standard lengths for papers in the academic world, depending upon the discipline. For example, in many biblical studies, theology and religion, and arts and humanities areas, published essays of 8,000–10,000 words are not uncommon (usually though not always including footnotes). But a paper that size is far too long for delivery in all but the most extreme circumstances. Some scholars recommend that you prepare two versions of the paper—one for reading and the other for publication. I don't recommend this. What I do recommend is that you prepare one paper, according to the terms of written publication, and then edit this paper down for delivery at the conference itself. This editing can be done in advance, or, if you are confident enough in your ability, you can do it on the occasion to conform to the parameters imposed.

In any case, a conference paper is a ready-made opportunity for publication. The requirement of preparing the paper for the conference ensures that there is a paper written. In this sense, this is perhaps as close as a scholar gets to the kinds of deadlines that were imposed during college and graduate school. That is also why I suggest that you should prepare the paper as close to the final form as possible. This means that all of the research should be done, and the footnotes written and included, so as to not need doing later. Then, once the conference is over and the few typographical errors have been corrected, any glaring weakness in the argument corrected, or a neglected source found and critiqued, the paper stands ready to publish—whether the conference proceedings are published or you submit the paper elsewhere. Once all of this work is done, there is no good reason not to publish the prepared conference paper.

Class Lectures

Professors often spend a large amount of time preparing and writing class lectures. Class lectures vary in the level of their detail, scholarship, and particularity, often depending upon the nature of the course and the goals of the professor. In North America, the educational system is usually geared toward a textbook approach to learning. Rather than students buying a number of discrete sources, often primary sources, there is a tendency in many subjects, certainly at the undergraduate level, to use one major textbook that brings together the various perspectives in the field and presents them in a systematic and coherent way. I often hear colleagues complain, however, that they cannot find just the right textbook for their course, and as a result they have to provide in their own lectures what is deficient in the textbook. A useful solution to the problem is to prepare class lectures that can be transformed into a suitable book, perhaps even a textbook for this particular course and other courses that are like it.

There was a time in higher education when professors would come to class and read their lectures to their students. The German term for lecture, *Vorlesung*, captures this practice very well. Often these lectures were being read from a manuscript that would find its way into print. Some of these professors even corrected the manuscript as they were reading to their students. I am not suggesting that most of us should be doing this—not least because this is not the way that most of us teach or the way that most of our students learn. However, that does not mean that your class lectures cannot provide suitable material for a book. One of my books came directly from prepared course material. I prepared lectures for a number of different courses, including an introductory survey of the subject and more specialized courses on particular dimensions of the subject. As a result, I had a variety of lecture materials that I had used. These included broad surveys of material and more focused treatments of subjects and people. When the opportunity came along, I used this material as the basis for writing up these lectures into major sections of the textbook I coauthored with another scholar. The basis of much of his portion of the book had derived from similar material that he also had developed in the course of his teaching.

Class lectures can conceivably be transformed into a number of different types of publications, but one of the most readily apparent is a textbook that meets the needs of the very course that you are teaching. You can have some confidence that the textbook will be successful, because the material has already been productively tested in the classroom.

Supplementary Class Notes

Related to class lectures are supplementary class notes. A number of years ago I found myself teaching a course in which I was very happy with the textbook. The nature of the course did not lend itself to lecturing, so I was not working on developing class lectures for this particular group of students. The students, however, were far less satisfied with the textbook than I was. There were a number of reasons for this, not least that the textbook was written in Britain, and its British English style sometimes did not come across as reader-friendly as it might have. As a result, the students were repeatedly asking me to clarify various concepts and issues that were raised in the text. Then, as I tried to reread the textbook from the perspective of the student, I tried to anticipate their problems by coming up with some supplementary notes to guide them. These notes were originally meant simply as supplementary material. The next year I offered the same course again, although this time I changed textbooks. The textbook was different, but the students had heard of the supplementary notes and requested them, so this provided another opportunity to work on revising and expanding them. The upshot of this was that what began as a few supplementary notes to a difficult textbook became a full manuscript of a handbook to the subject in its own right. This book has been in print for fifteen years now and has sold several thousands of copies, and it continues to be used at a wide range of institutions.

Even something that might seem as ephemeral or course-sensitive as supplementary class notes might well have potential for being developed into a significant academic publication.

As I mentioned above, publishers must publish. They must publish if they wish to stay in business, because their primary business is the selling of journal subscriptions, monographs and other kinds of books, and the like. If a journal appears in four fascicles a year, with eight to ten articles in each fascicle, it has to publish thirty-two to forty articles every year. If a publisher's budget is formed around publishing a book a month in a particular series, that means that twelve accepted manuscripts must appear as printed books every year in order to meet that budget. If these publishers have to publish, they may as well be publishing my stuff and your stuff. As I have shown in this chapter, most academics are producing more than enough material to keep themselves and their publishers busy with new projects.

4

PICK YOUR POISON
Selection of a Publisher

When it comes right down to it, you may know all of the mechanics of writing a publishable piece, but until you identify a suitable publisher—in other words, pick your poison—and send the article or book manuscript to that publisher, you will not become a publishing scholar. There are many different types of publishers. These include, among others, popular or trade publishers that produce the books found in the major chain stores, university presses usually supported by their universities and a variety of grants and other forms of publishing subvention, a variety and range of academic publishers often with their own academic areas or preferred type of book, and a host of niche or specialty publishers that concentrate on a type or subject of book. For the most part, as an academic writer you will mostly be interested in university presses and academic publishers, although there are also some specialty publishers that offer possibilities.

Whatever the nature of the publishing house involved, there are two important factors to keep in mind regarding selection of a publisher: (1) you need to know the particular requirements of the publishers, and (2) you need to match the right potential publication with the right publisher.

Knowing the Publishers

One of the major obligations of an aspiring publishing scholar is to know the various avenues for potential publication. This kind of knowledge can only be gained by studying the particular publishers and their publications.

Let's take journals first. A prospective author should have an idea of how often a potential journal is published, the types of articles that it accepts (detailed studies or broad surveys, technical or popular level), the lengths of articles, the style expected in a submission, the general reputation in the field, and, in some ways most importantly, the amount of time you can expect before they return a verdict and, assuming the article is accepted, before it appears in print. There are some journals that want the author to write a letter of inquiry first (and even some nonscholarly journals that do not take submissions, but these can usually be dismissed), but most simply accept submissions any time. All of these factors are important considerations, because they may well influence which journals you select for submission of your articles. For example, if your tenure review is coming up in a year and a half, and the committee demands that the article be out and in its hands for review, but the journal you are considering takes six months for a response (sixth months to a year for an editorial yea or nay is not uncommon for journals and monograph series) and there is a two-year backlog, that journal—no matter how prestigious and important—is probably not the journal to go with at this time, if you want the article to figure positively into your tenure review. Often journals have obscure requirements that are particular to themselves. Some journals have not yet adjusted to the electronic age and still require that the author send a hard copy of the article, and even a computer disk with the electronic file on it. Others have a particular address to use for submission, even if the editorial offices are not at that location. You can only learn these things by studying each particular journal, but they are important items to note. Many journals will not return a rejected article, assuming in this day and age that everyone has a backed up hard and electronic copy.

Book publishers are similar in many respects. However, whereas virtually all journals want the complete article at the time of submission, usually including an electronic file, academic publishers vary in what they require. Some want a letter of inquiry first, while others want a letter and a proposal. Proposals vary from publisher to publisher, so you will need to find out what each one requires. Many publishers want a proposal package that consists of at least the following: title, author with brief summary of qualifications, envisioned audience, brief summary of the book, outline of contents, date of submission of final manuscript, and usually one or two chapters. The publisher will then probably ask for the entire manuscript if they are interested in pursuing it. Some publishers demand the full manuscript right from the start, especially from junior

scholars who do not have an established research profile. My own preference when I have edited monograph series is to request right from the start
an entire manuscript from a junior scholar. For a senior scholar, I may
accept a proposal on the basis of minimal paperwork, subject to delivery
of the final manuscript that fulfills expectations. There is no substitute
for checking on this required submission information in advance.

For both journal and book publishers, the expectation, except under
unusual circumstances, is that the submitted manuscript has not been
published before and that it is not concurrently being considered for publication by another publisher. This policy can often prove frustrating to
young scholars who are anxious to have their first book or major article
published. Many publishing companies and editorial boards are quite slow
in their evaluations of manuscripts, because of the reliance on volunteer
boards of scholars. So there is an understandable temptation to submit
a manuscript to multiple publishers. Because of the delays in response, a
few publishers are willing to assess a manuscript that has been submitted to more than one publisher if the author lets the publisher know from
the outset. I have never been comfortable with this policy, however. I as
editor have been burned on several occasions, where I have gone through
the entire process of finding a member of the editorial board to evaluate
a manuscript, pursuing them to receive their opinion, and then contacting the author, only to be told that they had submitted the manuscript
elsewhere and have decided to go with the other offer. I must admit that
it might be difficult to consider a submission graciously from this same
author in the future, knowing that the effort of assessing the manuscript
might be for naught.

Matching the Right Publication with the Right Publisher

Once you have studied the various publishers and know what they expect
and demand, it is important to match your potential publication with the
right publisher. There is no point in thinking that a publisher will publish
your article—even if it is the greatest manuscript on this topic ever written—if your article does not meet the parameters of what the publisher is
looking for. A colleague once said that the most important article that he
had written in the course of his academic career was a manuscript that
was somewhere in the neighborhood of 30,000 words long. That's about
seventy-five pages in print! It may have been an excellent article, but he
naturally had trouble getting it published, because most journals do not

accept articles of that length. Most of them are looking for articles closer to the 8,000–10,000 words range. If those are their parameters, an article of 30,000 words will never get accepted. I had an incident of this sort myself. A colleague and I coauthored an article and submitted it to one of the most prestigious journals in our field. We received notice back that the article was accepted but that it had to be reduced in length because this journal only accepted articles of 8,000 words, and our submission was somewhere around 10,500 words. This seemed reasonable enough, so we resubmitted the article reduced down to about 9,000 words. The editor responded by saying essentially that the 8,000 words was nonnegotiable and it would have to be no more than 8,000 words. We resubmitted again, this time at only about fifty words or so over 8,000. Again, we got the response that the article had to be under 8,000 words. We pulled the final few words out so that the article came in just a few words under 8,000, and now the editor was as pleased as could be. Did our cutting of these words make the article better? No, but it made the article shorter, and that journal only took articles no more than 8,000 words in length.

One of the noticeable features in my discussion is that the length of publications is usually referred to by publishers and editors in terms of the number of words involved, not the pages. The reason for this is obvious—people vary in the number of words that they put on the page. This number often ranges from 225 words to nearly 600 words, not counting the added confusion of calculating footnotes, which are often printed at a different size than the body of the text. As I mentioned in the previous chapter, 400 words per page is a reasonable estimate of the number of words on an average published page. You can of course calculate the number of words that a particular publisher gets on a page, but sometimes this varies depending on how a book might be designed. Nevertheless, by using the figure of 400 words per page, you can calculate with the word counter on your computer the number of pages of a published piece.

Length parameters are a common limitation on acceptance of an article, but there are other requirements that need to be followed as well, such as the proper referencing system. A colleague told me the story of an article he submitted to a particular journal. He was told that they would like to publish the article, but that they noticed that the article had no footnotes, and they thought that the article really needed footnotes to ensure that the points made were fully supported. My colleague was intrigued by this comment, as he had written the article without reference to any other scholarly literature or discussion and genuinely believed that he was making a unique contribution. Nevertheless, he realized that the issue of the footnotes might become a sticking point, so he went through the manuscript and added footnotes where he thought appropriate. These were not footnotes that indicated the sources of material used but were indications of other scholarly contributions that might be of interest to a reader. He submitted the revised article to the journal, and it was promptly accepted. He received a note back saying that they were sure that he would agree that the addition of the footnotes made for a much better article. He did not really think so, but it certainly made the editors of the journal happier.

One last point to reiterate here is that, because of the various constraints that publishers place on themselves, there are occasionally opportunities for publication that would otherwise not arise. Most journals have a fixed number of pages and a standard number of words per page. Journal publishers often find themselves with a few pages left over in a given fascicle of the journal. They might be able to sell some more advertising, but one thing that they almost assuredly will not do is leave the pages blank. This opens up the opportunity for scholars to produce short notices and brief articles that can jump the queue to the front of the line and fill a space that would otherwise cause problems. A colleague of mine started his publishing career by essentially providing short articles for a number of major journals. He soon accumulated a respectable list of publications.

There are a number of other factors that may enter into the decision of where to send an article or a book manuscript. Most academic fields such as biblical studies, theology and religion, and the arts and humanities are relatively small, with perhaps only a few thousand people at the core of most of these disciplines. This means that it is reasonable to get to know a good number of people in your particular field who might work for or with various publishers. Some of them may serve as advisors, while others may sit on various editorial boards. In any event, it is not unusual for authors to use their personal connections with various levels of acquaintance to enhance their possibilities of publication. At the end of the day, however, the key to getting an article or book published is that you first have to send an article or book manuscript to a publisher. There is no way around this.

5

PRESENTATION IS ALMOST EVERYTHING

Publishers, whether they are publishers of journals or of books, are some-times odd creatures. They have their own individual publishing styles, and they like to see and use these styles in their publications. Some of these particulars and, I dare say, peculiarities are driven by tradition, per-haps even nationalist pride. For example, British publishers tend to like single quotation marks (what they sometimes affectionately call "inverted commas") and put them (usually, though not always—believe it or not, there are extensive rules for these things) inside the closing punctuation mark, such as a comma or period ("full stop," they would call it). Some are a matter of tradition, or perhaps even wanting to be different from someone else. Major university presses disagree over whether words such as *particulariz/se* should use *z* or *s* in the spelling. In that sense, both are good British spellings (or bad or troublesome British spellings). Some publishers like to include full publishing information in the footnotes or endnotes, including city, publisher, and date, while others simply want the city or even just the date. Some use a host of Latin words, such as ibid., loc. cit., op. cit., and the like; others use short titles; while others use something else. Some publishers like full names of authors, while others like initials for first names, and some want small caps for sur-names, while others do not. Continental European publishers are perhaps the most unusual in some of their preferences, such as odd punctuation or continual cross-referencing in footnotes to the first mention of a work. In other words, despite what you may have been taught in high school, col-lege, or even graduate school, there simply is not a single, unitary, and— certainly not—correct way of writing and submitting a paper or book manuscript, insofar as the style of the publishers is concerned. However, there is a single, unitary, and correct way of presenting an article, chapter, or book manuscript to a particular publisher—that is their way. And these publishers let you know what it is.

In light of this situation, there are a number of considerations that you should attend to in preparing your written manuscript for presentation to the publisher. These include (1) giving reasons for publishers to say "yes" to your manuscript, (2) following every stylistic detail as closely as possible, (3) paying attention to some of the most important details, (4) not trying to become a typesetter, (5) knowing about CRC, (6) paying attention to spelling and grammar, and (7) writing the cover letter.

Give Reasons for Publishers to Say "Yes," Not "No"

As an author, you need to give the publisher every reason for saying "yes" to your submission, rather than giving the publisher excuses to say "no."

Think about this for a minute. If you were the lofty editor of an important journal or monograph series (you may already be, or may well become one, and may wish to remember some of the thoughts and feelings you had as you contemplated this), how would you respond if you received a potential article manuscript that completely disregarded the format in which you wanted it submitted? Let's say that your journal only considers hard copy submissions accompanied by a disk with the electronic file, written in 14-point type double spaced on the page. Instead, you receive an e-mailed pdf file (of course, preceded by a very kind cover letter begging you to consider the attached article) of a manuscript in 10-point single-spaced type. This gives you every reason in the world simply to push the return button on your computer and say, "Sorry, we don't consider submissions of this sort." Fast, efficient, and done—rejection. Such a form of rejection—and it no doubt does happen, believe me (more on that in the following chapter)—does not even get to the issue of whether the article has any academic or intellectual merit. The submission was obviously written by someone who had not bothered to take time to conform the manuscript to the standards of your particular journal.

Despite the apparent arbitrariness of the various presentation styles used by publishers, there is usually at least a rationale for why they want what they want. You as a potential author need to know what it is and do it. You want the editor to be favorably disposed toward your article at least initially, and put it into the system for serious evaluation. You want your article considered on the basis of its scholarly merits, not on the basis of a poor first impression. In my experience, editors often want tangible reasons to reject articles—after all, they receive far more manuscripts than they can publish. The sloppy or haphazard or inattentive appearance of the manuscript is, at least in some minds, a good enough reason for contemplating rejection—with specific evidence that can be pointed to, such as the incorrect footnote form, spelling errors, etc.[1] Who can blame editors for thinking that sloppy presentation reflects sloppy scholarship? It is a natural logical leap. Most editors find it far more difficult, at least psychologically, to reject a manuscript that is presented word perfectly and in the exact style of the journal. After all, the author must know something about what he or she is talking about if time was taken to conform the article exactly to the parameters of the journal—and think of all of the time that will be saved in production of the article if the typesetter (who works from the author's nicely prepared electronic file) has very little to do to get it ready to send out for proofreading. These are reasons for acceptance of the article. Of course, we always hope that the ultimate decision will be made on the basis of the content and quality of the argument, but we also know the reality of the publishing environment—there are a variety of other, less tangible reasons that enter into decisions. If the decision comes down to a choice between two equally meritorious articles, the one that is presented in conformity with the parameters of the press will certainly have the advantage. And in getting published, you want every advantage on your side.

In my experience, the only ones who regularly ignore the self-evident truthfulness of what I have said regarding presentation are senior scholars. Senior scholars, when they submit articles to journals or chapters for collections or even manuscripts for monograph series, regularly ignore the conventions of the individual publishing companies. I know, because I have had to receive and then deal with their work. It is very difficult to tell a senior scholar, "We would like to publish your manuscript, but please revise it according to our house style," when you know that they may simply take it to another publisher who will gladly accept it, physical deformities and all. One of the reasons why senior scholars are sometimes neglectful of the style of individual publishers is that—apart from the obvious sense of superiority they may believe their position in the discipline warrants—they have been preparing their manuscripts this way for some time, and they cannot be bothered to change to another method just for this one piece that they are doing for you. I have some sympathy for this argument—that is perhaps why I simply shrug and start editing such manuscripts when I receive them—especially as I still sometimes receive submissions from scholars who have not yet learned how to use computers (I really do!). I realize that most of us can operate computers, including using computers with software that can change the format of our manuscripts, such as the footnote style and information, but there are still scholars for whom the transition from typewriter to computer has been traumatic and not fully overcome. The fact that you are reading this book, however, probably indicates that you are not one of those senior scholars, so I would suggest that you take the time to conform your manuscripts to the house styles of the publications to which you are submitting them. This stylistic information can be found in any number of places. For journals, it is often found in a copy of the journal itself, or on a convenient Web site. Some journals include the basic submission information in each fascicle, while others list the information in at least one of the fascicles each year. For publishing houses for monograph series and other books, the information can be readily found on their Web sites. Some journals and publishers simply refer to standard style guides.

Many of the publishers in biblical studies, theology and religion, and the arts and humanities use a variation on the style presented in one of the following reference works. I advise you to learn which one is the most important for your particular discipline or disciplines and buy a copy to have handy for use. These guides often include more than simply the format for a complex footnote. They include lists of abbreviations of all sorts, and other often-useful arcane knowledge.

The standard works include the following:

University of Chicago Press Staff, eds., *The Chicago Manual of Style*, 15th ed. (Chicago: University of Chicago Press, 2003).

> This is a 984-page guide to the style developed by the staff of the University of Chicago Press, one of the best-known university publishers. They treat a wide range of possible writing and publishing situations, especially for arts, humanities, and theology/religion disciplines. This has become the standard guide to referencing in many publishing circles. This guide is also available online (http://www.chicago manualofstyle.org/).

Patrick Alexander et al., eds., *The SBL Handbook of Style: For Ancient Near Eastern, Biblical, and Early Christian Studies* (Peabody, Mass.: Hendrickson, 1999).

> This 280-page guide has established itself as the standard style guide for many areas of ancient study, especially of the Bible.

Joseph Gibaldi, ed., *MLA Handbook for Writers of Research Papers*, 6th ed. (New York: Modern Language Association of America, 2003).

> This 361-page guide is the standard for those writing in language-based disciplines, such as English and other literatures. One of its recent innovations is to include more on citation of electronic sources.

Kate L. Turabian, *A Manual for Writers of Research Papers, Theses, and Dissertations*: *Chicago Style for Students and Researchers*, 7th ed. (rev. Wayne C. Booth, Gregory G. Colomb, Joseph M. Williams, and University of Chicago Press Editorial Staff; Chicago: University of Chicago Press, 2007).

> This 488-page guide is a "shortened" form of the *Chicago Manual of Style* for students. Many educational institutions insist upon the use of "Turabian" by students in their presentation of papers. The institution that benefits most from this is no doubt the University of Chicago Press.

Follow Every Stylistic Detail as Closely as Possible

There are numerous details to take into account in preparing a manuscript for publication. If you ever have the chance to see the marked copy that has been prepared by a professional copy editor for the typesetter, you will see that there are no details left to chance. Even then, a good copy editor must often make a number of decisions specifically for the particular manuscript that is being edited, as every manuscript is different and requires some special treatment.

Even though you probably do not want to become a copy editor (it is a noble profession, and my wife worked as one for a number of years, so I have come to love and respect at least one of them),[2] that does not mean that you cannot and should not learn many of the details of preparing a manuscript—knowing that you will never get all of them correct. Nor should you attempt to become a typesetter through use of your personal computer—but more on that below.

There are two types of house style details that you should become familiar with and try to follow as closely as you can for any particular publisher to whom you are submitting work: macro and micro features of the manuscript.

The first is the set of macro-manuscript features. These are the basic parameters that are important in preparing a manuscript. Most publishers tend to follow the same general set of rules in this regard (and differ far more greatly on the micro-manuscript features), but these should definitely be kept in mind, because they can be addressed relatively easily. These macro-manuscript features include such elements as the following:

- Whether the publisher accepts submissions via hard copy and/or electronic or soft copy, or hard copy followed by electronic, or electronic followed by hard copy

- The form in which the electronic copy is sent, whether by disk or CD-ROM or attachment, with or without an accompanying pdf

- The size, type, and kind of paper for a hard copy submission (yes, some publishers try to insist upon use of European A4 paper, not just standard North American 8 1/2 × 11 inch)

- Type size (either 12 or 14 point is pretty standard)

- Font style (Times New Roman is a good one to use if nothing is specified)

- Line spacing, by either single, double, or single-and-a-half spacing, or by leading (the space between the lines) by points, such as 15 or 17 points

- The widths of margins, which may vary for left and right or top and bottom, depending upon where the editor likes to write comments

- Whether a header or footer with or without page numbers should be used.

These are the major macro-manuscript features to make sure that your manuscript follows. Most publishers are fairly standard on these, but it pays to check in advance.

Micro-manuscript features are more complex. They include the kinds of nitty-gritty details that truly differentiate publishers from each other, and distinguish the attentive from the inattentive author. The kinds of micro-manuscript features that publishing houses often consider crucial include the following:

- Levels of headings within the article, such as title, major headings, and subheadings, and how many levels of specificity they go down

- Styles of headings within the article, such as whether all headings are aligned to the left margin or whether the title and major headings are centered and others aligned left, etc.

- Whether the manuscript should be submitted with footnotes or endnotes, sometimes with the endnotes in a separate electronic file (regardless of whether the notes are actually printed as footnotes or not)

- The notation style, whether social-scientific or traditional, or a style unique to the publisher

- Whether only citation or a mix of citation and content footnotes is used, and how this relates to the use of social-scientific notation style, if used

- Whether a bibliography is required if the social science method is not used (usually not for an article, but quite often for a book)

- Whether footnotes should be spaced the same as the main text or not (some publishers like footnotes single spaced even if the main body of the text is double spaced)

- The kind of information and the level of completeness of the footnote material, such as whether place of publication, publisher, date, series, and the like are or are not included and where they are included

- How first and subsequent references are handled in notes, such as short titles; the use of ibid., loc. cit., etc.; or a parenthetical reference to where the first full note is used, to name a few

- Abbreviations to use throughout the manuscript, both for sources and for standard English and Latin abbreviations, etc. (or et cetera).

These are some—but certainly not all—of the major micro-manuscript features.

Most of the comments above, while focused primarily on journal manuscript submissions, are also pertinent to submission of book manuscripts. A few extra considerations for book manuscripts are the following:

- Whether the preliminary pages should be in one or separate files

- How much detail is included in the preliminary pages, such as bibliographical information, half title page (the right-hand page before the title page), and dedication

- What the preliminary pages can or should include, such as a preface, foreword, and introduction or one or two of the above

- At what stage indexes and what types of indexes are included, and who is expected to compile them.

The publishing of a book can often include more variation and freedom in style, as each book is treated as an entity in its own right, rather than as one small part of a larger whole.

Those who master the above details for each publisher are going to be at least one step ahead of those who do not. Furthermore, once you train yourself to observe and implement these various stylistic rules, you will also help yourself significantly in your role as editor of volumes of others' essays.

Pay Attention to Some of the Most Important Details

The section above has given the broad parameters for the macro- and micro-manuscript features. Here are a few specific issues to pay attention to so that your manuscript can be submitted as close to the ideal of the publishing company as possible.

- British or American spelling? Most publishers use one or the other, although some Canadians try to maintain Canadian spelling (which is somewhere halfway between that of the USA and Britain). Even within British spelling, there may be some further distinctions, such as whether words end in *-ize* or *-ise*.

- Use of italics and underlining. These two are used synonymously in much copyediting parlance, so some publishers want authors not to use italics (because sometimes they can be missed) but to use underlining that will then be converted to italics. Others want italics to be used for all underlined material.

- Use of bold font and other odd forms of letters. Most publishers want authors to avoid use of bold font and other such contrivances, such as shadowing, reverse letters, or the like. These are merely time-consuming annoyances for the publisher to have to take out and replace with something else. If textual material needs to be emphasized, it should be italicized, and if it needs to be emphasized more than that, it should probably be rewritten.

- Punctuation. Most publishers follow either American or British punctuation, which becomes most obvious in terms of quoted material. In most contexts in American punctuation, the quotation marks fall outside of the punctuation when it is a comma or period, but inside semicolons, colons, and exclamation marks. Some British publishers turn this around and want the inverted commas (which usually begin with single rather than double as in the USA) within the punctuation. There are some British publishers, however, who have a far more complex set of rules that have the punctuation outside the inverted commas if a sentence or less is cited, but have the inverted commas outside the punctuation if more than a complete sentence is cited. If a publisher rejects your manuscript on the basis of getting this wrong, don't despair—immediately go to another publisher who is less obsessive-compulsive and far less likely to be institutionalized because of the obsession. In my experience, few publishers are consistent in these rules anyway.

- Avoidance of extreme punctuation. Whatever you do!!! avoid using multiple punctuation marks, right?? Exclamatory and dramatic punctuation is never a substitute for good writing.

- Citation data in footnotes. Many North American scholars are bred on the idea of providing complete footnote information, such as place (even multiple places), publisher, and date, along with series information. Many European publishers do not want such complete information but want only place or date. I prefer to have complete information, as simply the date tells nothing about the nature of the publication, and the place, especially when it is London or New York, does not really help in finding the publisher (this convention stems from a time when all publishers were located in the big publishing cities). Nevertheless, this is the preference of some publishers. You may wish, before you delete the extraneous information that a publisher does not require, to save the complete information for your own future reference if you do not have this in another form or file.

Paying attention to a number of these issues will help to ensure that the manuscript you submit to a publisher will be given its due recognition, rather than being stopped at the door because of its failure to show that you cared enough to get to know your prospective publisher.

Don't Try to Become a Typesetter

A friend of mine was working on a book with another scholar. This scholar seemed to think that he was a typesetter, or perhaps he was a frustrated typesetter who had never had his dreams realized. In any case, as they were working together, the frustrated typesetter would send his portion of the manuscript to my friend for compiling of the larger manuscript. The material that was sent virtually always contained all sorts of formatting and hidden commands that needed to be stripped out. The problem was aggravated by the fact that when the frustrated typesetter sent revised material, this material again came with all of the original formatting and hidden commands within it, even if my friend had sent the manuscript back stripped of these commands. The frustrated typesetter may have thought that all of these buried bells and whistles made his manuscript look better (and perhaps it did for an easily impressionable group of undergraduates), but it only led to heightened frustration for my friend as he constantly and repeatedly stripped such commands out.

The reason to minimize such extra formatting is that publishers usually want a basic manuscript (even text only) with no more commands in it than are necessary, because they will have to strip them out themselves. The kinds of commands to take out include such things as the following:

- Styles. All of the styles will be stripped out by the publisher who will then impose their own styles on the manuscript.

- Overuse of different fonts. The manuscript is best presented in one font throughout, except where ancient languages or other alphabets may be used (in that case, learn your publisher's views on transliteration).

- Overuse of formatting of headings and the like. The headings should be in the same font, size, and format as the rest of the manuscript, with centering of headings and other items kept to a minimum.

No matter how clever you may be with a computer, or how much of a typesetter you may think that you are, unless this is actually what you do as a vocation, you cannot hope to do the job as well or the way that the publisher wants it done. So don't even try. Your restraint will save you time in preparing the manuscript and save a lot of grief on the publisher's side as well.

What Is CRC? Can I Prepare It?

CRC refers to camera-ready copy. With the advent of computers, and the increased costs of typesetting, a number of publishers went to the process by which authors were invited to prepare CRC, or copy that could be directly used by the publisher for publication. In its early use, authors submitted their dot matrix or laser-printed manuscripts, and the publishers printed the books directly from these, with the title and bibliographical information page (usually, but not always) provided by the publisher. Most of the early manuscripts prepared in this way looked pretty awful then and look even worse now. My earliest CRC manuscript was probably better than most prepared at the time, but now obviously has some clear faults, as in those early stages some fonts were not compatible and introduced spacing problems and the like. On the basis of my working for a publisher, and working alongside my wife, I have continued to prepare some CRC manuscripts for publishers (in some cases, I would receive a larger royalty for having prepared the CRC). My recent efforts cannot be distinguished from what would be prepared by the publishers themselves, because many publishers now use freelance typesetters who work from their own computers at home, doing just what my wife used to do and what I myself have done.

The fact that readers cannot tell the difference between manuscripts that I have prepared and those prepared by others does not mean that preparing CRC is easy to do. It is not. Most of the time, almost anybody can recognize a manuscript that was prepared by an author. These stand out for any number of reasons—the most obvious being that the people preparing them do not know what they are doing but think that because they can use the computer they can be typesetters. Do they know what kerning is? What about leading? Have they put in a hard space, or should they? Is a loose line a moral problem? What are the house rules of hyphenation (rules the automatic hyphenation function does not follow)? What are en dashes and em dashes? How do you treat widows and orphans in a responsible way?[3] These are just a few of the obvious things that most people have no clue about.

Many publishers still use or even require authors to prepare CRC. In many such cases, the publishers no longer use a printed CRC produced by the author but ask the author to prepare the manuscript using an electronic template provided by the publisher, or whose parameters are given to them by the publisher. Then, when the manuscript is prepared in this electronic form, the publisher sends the electronic file to the printer and the book is printed from the electronic file. This method is increasingly being utilized, especially by publishers who are utilizing print on demand. In other words, rather than simply printing a large number of books in advance and then storing them until they are sold, these print-on-demand publishers print only the number of books that are ordered and paid for, and to do so they use the electronic file. Some of the advantages of this electronic method of preparing manuscripts are that this requires far less paper and possibility of physical problems (if it is laid out properly in the electronic file), and the file can be retained for future printings and reprintings. However, just as with preparation of printed CRC, the finished quality depends on the preliminary quality of the work and attention to detail of the author. There are numerous features that give an author away, besides horrific misspellings that slip through (or, more amusingly, the correctly spelled wrong word that the spell check did not pick up). One of the most frequent of these difficulties is caused by font incompatibility and substitution. This occurs when a number of fonts are used in a file and the printer does not have the same font matches, and so substitution occurs (this can happen with any electronic manuscript prepared by a publisher). I have unfortunately had this occur, where, in the midst of some elegant argument, there is a weird squiggle. The fact that no one has ever asked me what this squiggle is bothers me even more.

If given a choice, I would suggest that only the rare and meticulous author prepare CRC, as there are a number of technical details to learn and many ways in which the whole thing can go disappointingly wrong so that the resulting work looks far less competent than it should.

A Word on Spelling and Grammar

Until now, I have not made a special point in this chapter of mentioning spelling or grammar. I am assuming that the author will only submit work that has been thoroughly checked for both spelling and grammar. Only letter-perfect manuscripts should be submitted—recognizing that it is nearly impossible to prepare such a manuscript.

There are a couple of warnings that I would like to issue, however. One is that many authors, who grew up on and have perhaps only really used computers for creating their written work, have never learned to proofread hard copy in printed form. I have only met a couple of people whom I considered to be proofreaders on-screen at the level of proofreaders of hard copy. Most who rely upon proofreading by reading on-screen produce material that is full of all sorts of mistakes and errors. These include spelling errors, grammatical mistakes, double spaces after major punctuation, and even formatting mistakes that are missed because such readers cannot see any more than a page or portion of a page at a time on the screen (despite their ability to preview more if they wish).

The second warning is that far too many authors rely upon the spell-check and grammar-check functions of their computers—and produce error-filled manuscripts. I remember reviewing a book on the use of computers in humanities subjects. The book waxed lyrical and at length about the virtues and innumerable strengths of using a computer in humanities scholarship—and there are undeniable benefits. One of these virtues, expatiated upon, was that there was no need to produce manuscripts with any spelling errors in them any longer. This chapter was filled not with spelling errors in the sense of grossly misspelled words but with spelling errors where the wrong word is correctly spelled. So I was reading *there* for *their*, and *its* for *it's*, and the like. The same can be said for grammar. The grammar check may identify too many uses of the passive voice, but it cannot be a judge of good or bad style.

I would suggest that before you try to edit and proofread on-screen, you first thoroughly master editing and proofreading of hard copy. I do not mean by this doing it once and thinking that you have mastered it, but learning to proofread until flawless manuscripts are produced every time.

Writing the Cover Letter

Many works on writing for publication spend a lot of time with what I consider relatively minor issues of presentation, such as preparing the cover letter. Some of them even give samples and print copies of these letters in the book. I think that this is a waste of paper (unlike my advice to edit hard copy, above). I suggest that any cover letter should have five essential elements, presented in a clear business letter format, even if sent by e-mail:

- An address to the correct person by title

- An initial statement asking the editor to consider the enclosed or attached manuscript (give its title) for publication

- An assurance that the manuscript is not being considered by another publisher (I think this is the best policy—see discussion on p. 69)

- Clear contact information including both traditional and electronic addresses

- Your academic position, if available, with your closing signature.

Most editors do not spend great amounts of time perusing cover letters, except to make sure they have contact information for the author. Be sure that the contact information is clear and decipherable. I would even consider putting it on the manuscript.

Despite these words of wisdom, there are always some who will provide far too much information and the wrong things in a cover letter. Here are several elements not to include in such a cover letter: an expansive discussion of the topic of the manuscript (let the manuscript speak for itself), the history of the origins of the manuscript (who cares? well, you might, but the publisher does not), how qualified you are to treat such a topic (if it does not come out in the manuscript, your self-congratulatory autobiography won't help), a disclaimer on what you have not done in your manuscript or a list of its deficiencies, an apology for not doing another kind of work, a disclosure that you are anything but a competent scholar in the field, and a statement that indicates that the publisher will not have exclusive initial rights to publication. Any one of these may well turn the editor against you and your manuscript or may even lead to outright rejection. The one possible exception to the above is that, if you are submitting a dissertation, some editors do appreciate receiving a short description of what things you think you need to do to make your manuscript into a publishable book—if you have not made these changes already! Your recognition that you need to take out the literature survey and rewrite the opening chapter to set the stage may help show that you have an informed view of the difference between a dissertation and a readable monograph. My one caution here is that the list of changes not be too excessive, but that the items be defined and relatively easily doable so that you can submit the final, revised manuscript as soon as possible if requested.

Sometimes editors will ask you for recommendations of people to offer an opinion on your manuscript. If the editor does so, by all means provide such people—and make sure they are people who know your work and will probably speak highly of it.

I think that the shorter the cover letter the better. The work itself must be the focus of evaluation.

There are many reasons why an editor may ultimately reject a manuscript for publication. I would make every effort to ensure that I give the editor as few reasons as possible for doing so. This means eliminating every possible technical error—it should go without saying that spelling and grammar mistakes are simply unacceptable—but more than that, conforming the manuscript to the recommended house style of the publisher. Attention to such detail creates an atmosphere of acceptance, because it shows that the author has taken the time to find out, learn, and then apply the style of the publisher to the particular written piece. This not only eliminates an obvious reason for rejection of the manuscript—the person is sloppy and lazy and has produced a clearly error-ridden piece of work—but it creates confidence that, if the author has taken the time in these matters, surely the content must be equally attentive to detail and warrant consideration. Even if not every one of your articles or book manuscripts is accepted because it looks good, at least you know that you have presented the very best representation of your scholarship. The editor knows this, too.

6

HANDLING REJECTION—IT WILL COME

The only authors who have probably not suffered the emotional pain of rejection are those who have never submitted their work to an editor. And it can hurt. There is no doubt that there is a sharp sting that is felt when you open up the envelope (probably not even returning the manuscript) and receive a rejection letter from an editor. I have received numerous rejection letters. I wish now that I had saved them all. It's not that they would have been large enough in number to paper a wall, but they would have provided some interesting reading later in my career, especially now that it is more usual for editors to ask me to submit something rather than for me to send out an unsolicited manuscript. Now when I think back on all of the rejection letters that I have received, I have forgotten the various curses that I uttered at the time, the vows of revenge that I swore to fulfill, and the commitment to do something awful to these editors if our paths ever crossed in the future or I ever was on the other side of the table and able to inflict pain on them (I have actually been in such a position and conveniently had memory lapses regarding who these people had been). Receiving rejection letters is a natural part of the writing and submitting process. Welcome it as a necessary step in becoming a publishing and contributing scholar.

From this process, there are a number of lessons that can be learned to help make you a better author. I handle these under the following categories: (1) recognize the limitations of a rejection letter, (2) learn from the rejection letters where possible, (3) take advantage of the opportunity to resubmit, and (4) learn to be a critical self-editor.

Recognize the Limitations of a Rejection Letter

A rejection letter does not necessarily reflect on the quality of your work.[1] Now, I want to say this gently, but it may be that your work is absolutely awful, flawed in its argumentation, without a thesis, and poorly documented, if documented or argued at all. However, I doubt that you would be reading this book if your work was that bad. You probably would simply be harassing editors and publishers with more flawed and hopeless articles. In that case, I would suggest that you consider another line of work entirely.

Instead, I have noted above that there are all sorts of reasons for rejection that do not necessarily reflect on the quality of the work submitted. One of the major reasons is that the peer-review process is inherently and fundamentally flawed. It may be the best system that we have developed, but it is still flawed and does not actually always identify the best work. Sometimes the work submitted simply does not fit the parameters of the journal or publisher to which it is submitted, so that no matter how many times you keep revising and resubmitting the manuscript to that publisher it will be rejected. Then there are all sorts of political issues at stake. You may be taking a minority or out-of-favor position—even if it is ultimately proved to be correct. Or—perhaps I shouldn't even suggest this—it may be that your particular journal is trying to appeal to another language group. They have received enough publications in English and now want more in French or German, to make sure that some arbitrary or supposed balance is maintained (have you considered having your article translated into French?). Or perhaps your journal wants more articles from underrepresented groups. Short of changing your name, or renting a postal address in another part of the world, there is nothing you can do about these situations—and they have absolutely nothing to do with the quality of your work.

I have had plenty of experiences where I have had an article rejected, only to have the very same article accepted by another journal of equal or even higher quality. I remember one episode early in my career. I was meticulous in how I prepared the manuscript and thought that, on the basis of the publishing profile of this journal, my article would be one that they would accept. It was a shorter article by their standards, and I also noticed that they had a section for articles of this rough length. I sent it off but then received a letter back, rejecting it. The editor gave a couple of reasons, such as that they thought that the argument was not convincing. I looked at the several troublesome passages and decided I could fine-tune my arguments, without changing anything of substance. Then I found a journal that was at least as prestigious as the first and decided to send it to that journal. I made sure that I took the time to conform the article to the standards of this new journal—it was a European journal and so had a number of peculiarities not regularly used in English-speaking countries—and sent it off. The article was accepted without major changes and appeared in due course.

On another occasion, I prepared a response to a recent publication by a senior scholar. I sent this response to a journal that had some connection to the scholar to whom I was responding, apparently mistakenly thinking that interest in his positions would help my chances of publication. I soon received a letter back indicating several points that the journal found unconvincing, as rationale for rejection. I realize now that, since the former editor of the journal was a close colleague of the scholar to whom I was responding, I probably should not have assumed that this connection would help my chances of publication. Instead, I made a few small changes and sent the article to another journal of at least as much prestige, and it was accepted and published forthwith. The scholar to whom I responded made sure in a subsequent publication that he directly addressed my objections to his work. The journal that accepted this second article was the same one that had originally rejected the first article mentioned above. So now I had published in two of the three journals to which I originally submitted these two articles, both with very high standing. I am confident that there was nothing wrong with the quality of either article, and the fact that each continues to be cited and responded to on the basis of their arguments is sufficient proof for me.

Learn from the Rejection Letters Where Possible

The kinds of rejection letters that you as an author might receive will vary, sometimes greatly. Some of these letters will prove to be very helpful, while others will not. Unfortunately, most of them will not. It will be up to you to decide which ones make positive contributions that are worth pursuing, and which ones provide nothing. There are a number of reasons that editors send such unhelpful letters. One of these is the pragmatic reason that they do not want to give you too much information about what is wrong with your manuscript because then you may actually revise it—and then what are they going to do with it? You come back to the editor and tell her that you have now corrected or changed everything she suggested, and she may feel undue pressure to publish the article or book when she really doesn't want to publish it at all. So in that case, it is simply easier to leave the comments vague and discourage any type of response on your part. A second reason that editors' comments are sometimes so unhelpful is that the editor himself has not actually read what you wrote but is simply summarizing what some other reviewer has written to him. Not having firsthand knowledge makes it more difficult to summarize the report that the editor received and to pass it along to you. Rather than say something inaccurate, most editors will simply say less or nothing. A third reason that editors sometimes do not want to give much detailed criticism in their rejection letters might be that, although they do not want to publish the article or book, they don't want anyone else to do it either, so if they give you helpful comments you may go elsewhere with it. If you go elsewhere and publish your work, and it ends up being a big success (and it may well, as editors often don't really know what will and won't catch on), then they look . . . well, you get the idea. It is better simply to discourage you and let you figure it out for yourself.

In the course of my writing career, there are numerous types of letters that I have received or have written rejecting an article or book manuscript. Despite what I have said above, there are things to be learned from virtually all of these letters, especially if the letters have been sent by conscientious editors who take their task seriously and want to be helpful. Let me characterize the types of rejection letters and what can be learned from them.

Short and Not So Sweet

The first type of rejection letter is the short letter that tells the author absolutely nothing. It usually begins by thanking the author for the submission but says that the article cannot be accepted. Often regret is expressed, but there are no substantive reasons given, apart from the fact that the piece did not seem to fit their publishing requirements. This type of letter gives very little information and hence has very little value in actually evaluating the article that you have written. If you have done a reasonably good job of shaping your submission to the requirements of the journal or publisher, have written what by your and others' accounts is a pretty good manuscript, and still get this kind of letter, you may wish to follow up with a further inquiry to ask if there is anything more that the editor can tell you. Some editors do not put everything forward in their initial letter, because they do not think that authors always want to hear more detailed bad news; however, they are sometimes willing to give more information when asked. If they do not, then don't become a pest by hounding the editor. You may wish to submit there again.

Technical Response

A second letter type includes all of the formal elements noted above but concentrates upon technical issues, including both elements of presentation, such as footnotes and layout, and elements of argument. A letter such as this can be quite helpful for a number of reasons. One of these is that it serves as a reminder that editors are sensitive to the importance of their particular house style, and they like to see it used in their publications. Despite the appearance of arbitrariness in the selection of house styles, most publications defend their house style on the basis of a complex of reasons. Some of these are nationalistic in origin (single quotation marks for British English, double carat marks for Spanish, etc., by virtue of who they are as a language group), while others are set by tradition or convention (-*ize* versus -*ise* is debated still in the UK) or something else. These need to be acknowledged to guarantee success in publishing, and a letter such as this comes as a reminder. More helpful, of course, are comments regarding the nature of the argument that you have developed, and places where it is lacking or needs further support. Sometimes this can be remedied by simply adding a footnote here or there, while at other times it may require a recasting of a paragraph, a section, or even an entire chapter. If an editor has taken time to give such guidance, this can be very helpful in bringing the manuscript into publishable form.

Extended Comment

A third type of letter, while it includes most of the formal elements mentioned above, may also go into some kind of an extended critique of the content of what you have written. Here is where you have the possibility of very valuable material to consider. If the reader of the article has taken time to review the content of the manuscript itself, there is the possibility that the reader has found some element or elements of the manuscript that need to be rethought, revised, or supplemented. This form of a letter goes beyond the kinds of technical and argumentative comments mentioned in the second type of letter above, and shows that the person who reviewed the manuscript has subject expertise and is willing to share it with you as the potential author. One thought to keep in mind is that this reviewer, of course, has a particular bias and orientation to the subject matter also. It may be that you have cited this author unfavorably in your own manuscript, or that the person is working in the same area and has arrived at a very different set of conclusions, or even that the person simply sees the subject in a different way than you have. Nevertheless, the fact that the person is willing to give advice in terms of the content—whether it is in terms of unknown, missed, or not sufficiently appreciated primary or secondary sources, etc.—provides further material for thought and possible incorporation into a revised form of the manuscript. This kind of helpful response is invaluable.

Invitation to Resubmit

A fourth letter allows for resubmission of the article. It is not usual to be allowed to resubmit a manuscript to a publisher that responds with an outright rejection, even if you follow it up with a request for more information. In fact, there are some publishers who simply do not allow or work with resubmissions. There are several reasons for this. An obvious reason is that some publishers believe that if the author could not get the work right the first time, it will never, even after revision, become the kind of piece that they want to publish. In other words, they believe that they should be publishing a type of work that is excellent from the start, and that a revised mediocre piece can never attain to that level of excellence, so there is no point in allowing a revised version to be resubmitted. Another reason why some publishers do not allow resubmission is that they believe that it unfairly obligates them to accept the revised piece for publication. The only potential unfairness is if they tell you what specifically you need to do to have your revised manuscript accepted for publication and then do not do so if the conditions are met. For example, an editor may say that your manuscript was seen to be deficient in three areas, and if you are able to fix these three areas by doing certain things (adding bibliography, recasting paragraphs, editing the style, or whatever they may be), then they would be willing to reconsider it for publication. If you do these things, the editor is placed in the situation of feeling compelled to accept the revised work. Otherwise the editor has to come back and say that you have indeed made these changes, but now you need to make other changes—and the process becomes interminable, as well as very costly in terms of time and effort. A third reason that some publishers do not accept revisions is that it takes a lot of time and energy. Some of these editors feel guilty (editors feel a lot of guilt about a lot of things; perhaps some should feel a bit more) that they need to have the manuscript refereed again before publication. The question is whether they go back to the same reviewer as before—who may or may not be favorably inclined to the piece, having reviewed it once—or go to a new reviewer, who may come up with a whole new set of judgments. I have had experience with all of these different editorial scenarios, on the basis of being an editor and an author, and such situations are not easy. As an editor, I have had a piece revised on the basis of an initial reader's comments, who was not able to review the manuscript the second time, only to be told by a new reviewer that there were all sorts of new alterations that needed to be made. I wish I had never allowed the resubmission.

An editor can say no to your manuscript in only so many ways in a rejection letter. Don't spend any more time than necessary psychologizing over the content by second-guessing yourself or reading insidious intent into the process, but take the letters for what they are and use them appropriately to make your manuscript better.

Take Advantage of the Opportunity to Resubmit

There is often pain associated with a letter of rejection, especially if it is curtly and briskly written without possibility of remedy, but also if it is one that allows for resubmission. Even if the letter from the editor allows for resubmission, there can also be a sting that comes along with the letter. Resubmission becomes an admission that our child was perhaps not as beautiful as we had thought it was—in fact, our baby may be in need of some fairly radical plastic surgery. That's a hard admission to make. Nevertheless, my advice is to take advantage of every opportunity for resubmission, rather than starting the submission process over again. If you choose to start over with a new publisher, you have to go through all of the work of conforming the manuscript to the parameters and guidelines of the new publisher, with the possibility of receiving the same or, perish the thought, an even worse letter back from the new publisher.

I had worked on an article for quite some time. It had begun as a conference paper delivered in a couple of different settings and then had been revised for submission to one of the most important journals in my primary field. I was very pleased with the article, as I thought that I had brought into play some new sources that had not been discussed in quite some time, and had developed a new perspective on several issues that I thought were very important. As a result, I submitted the article with some confidence to this prestigious journal. After the requisite wait, I received a letter in response. The letter was devastating. The letter was essentially a form of letter two mentioned above. It was not a critique of the substantive content of the article but a thorough and brutal critique of the technical dimensions of the article. Essentially, the letter from the editor said that I could not write and that this article was very poorly written in almost every imaginable way—and he had examples enumerated for several pages to show me that that was the case. Needless to say, I was pretty discouraged and had a choice to make. Part of me wanted to point out that I had several degrees in English, and I knew what I was doing and it could not be that bad anyway, and I would show him by taking the article to another publisher. I could have done that. However, I really wanted to publish in this particular journal, and the editor left open the opportunity to resubmit a completely rewritten manuscript. The encouragement was not strong, but he did say that he would be willing to look at it again if I thoroughly revised it. I observed that he did not say that he would accept it if I simply corrected all of the things that he had noted. He wanted the article thoroughly revised.

One of my closest friends and colleagues at the time was a major published poet and aspiring (and now highly successful) novelist and prose fiction writer. I showed him the article and the editor's response and, humbling myself (after all, did I mention that I have two degrees in English? and my friend did not at the time have a single degree in English—although he had already been anthologized alongside Robert Penn Warren, the Pulitzer Prize-winning American poet), asked him to take a look at my potential article, warts and all. Rather than siding with me against the editor, he immediately recognized the need for some serious recasting. We sat down with the article and worked through the entire thing over the course of a number of days, looking at each sentence in terms of how it was formed and how it contributed to the overall argument. My friend is, to say the least, very insightful, so when he would say something like, "I don't understand what you are saying," I had to take him seriously and ask myself whether I understood what I was saying. Often I did not, or if I did, I certainly had not expressed it well or clearly. After completing this time-consuming but rewarding process, I sent the article off for reconsideration. After a length of time, I received a letter saying that it had been accepted for publication. I have been gratified to note that, even nearly twenty years later, that article is still having an impact. A recent volume has noted that I provided a conclusive argument on a particular issue—one of the main topics I was arguing in the article. Taking the opportunity to resubmit the article was certainly the right thing to do—as was having a good friend who was willing to use his huge abilities to help me.

Learn to Be a Critical Self-Editor

Not everyone has access to an award-winning poet and best-selling novelist as a proofreader and stylist to help with preparing articles for publication. I know that I was fortunate in having my friend's help. However, to be honest, most articles published in scholarly journals and most monographs do not need award-winning prose to be more than adequate. But they do need to have decent prose to help make their case. This is where it is imperative that an aspiring author become a critical self-editor. Editing one's own material is one of the most difficult tasks to learn and to learn to do well.

There are all sorts of good reasons why people do not make good editors of their own writing. One of these is that we as authors know what the writing is supposed to say, having thought in advance about what the piece is to be about and then having executed the writing of it. Authors easily overlook the poor ways in which such thoughts, even if they are noble and good ones, are expressed in prose. A substantive and perceptible gap often exists between the intention of the author and the fulfillment of that goal in the actual writing. Another reason we are such poor editors of our own work is that we simply may not be very experienced in using, or not in complete control of, the basic tools of English composition. Many disciplines do not make high demands on developing writing abilities. This is even increasingly the case in humanities disciplines. As a result, many very competent academics are in areas where they are not required to develop excellent written English communication skills—and they don't. The result is often very poor prose, whether because it is boring and repetitious, or loose and undisciplined, or imprecise and abstract. A third major reason is that authors do not take time to edit their work. If the writer is not accomplished to begin with, it is unreasonable to expect that writer to be able to read and refine that same poor writing. Nevertheless, a writer needs to learn to be aware of when the prose is not working, and to do something about it to make it read more fluently and communicate more ably. Sometimes this requires not just editing but complete rewriting. This may seem like unnecessary labor, but there are occasions when editing simply will not do what needs to be done, and the author needs to undertake a thorough and complete rewriting of the manuscript. This means rethinking it from top to bottom and rewriting accordingly.

In the course of my experience as a writer and as an editor, I have had to deal with a number of key mistakes that authors make that should and could have been caught and remedied at an earlier stage of writing. I will lay out three of these for you as a developing author to beware of as you write and then rewrite your prose: structural problems, ponderous writing, and verbal retention. I will then provide some questions you may want to use to evaluate your writing in the self-editing process.

Structural Problems

One of the first and most important factors in good writing is structure. An author must keep an eye on the need for a clear outline of the overall shape of the piece and on the importance of the major and sometimes minor sections within it. I have often found that, if I am able to create a balanced outline of what I am going to say, it helps me both to organize my thoughts so that they are well-structured and laid out in advance, and to clarify my ideas and how they relate to each other. Once a well-considered outline has been developed, it is much easier to face the task of writing the entire manuscript. Writing the article, or even monograph, becomes more a matter of filling out the sections within the outline, guided by what has been said and being guided by what the next stage in the outline prescribes. The failure to use a good outline can result in very unstructured and even unbalanced composition. Sometimes it means that ideas are not organized in the best logical progression, or various ideas that would logically belong together are included simply at the place where the author thought of them or remembered to insert them. Another danger of not using a good outline is the creation of a misshapen final product. An outline helps to control the relative lengths of sections. One of the details that I often include in an outline is the length in words of any given literary unit. If an article is meant to be

8,000 words, and I have a brief introduction and then four sections before the conclusion, I may wish to allocate no more than 1,850 words to each section (and 400 words to the introductory first paragraph and 200 words to the conclusion). Within one of these major sections, if I have two or three minor points to make, I will also want to give them suitable and proportionate weight. This does not mean that each section has to be of equal length with another, but there is a sense in which balance needs to be maintained. That avoids the problem of writing 4,000 words on the first main point, only to have to get rid of half of that so that the other three points are not terribly underdeveloped. Remember also that a good use of signposts along the way will help guide your reader through your outlined structure.

Ponderous Writing

A second issue involves being too careful and meticulous in getting words out. One of the hindrances to good and productive writing can be the sense that every word that is put down on paper or input on-screen must be the well-considered and final word and cannot be altered. As a result, the writing process can often be slow and laborious, and often quite discouraging, and the final product can reflect such ponderousness. To counter this, I often encourage inexperienced writers to overwrite in their first draft. I tell these writers that they should simply sit down and write as much and as quickly as they can—following their outline, of course. If the writing is such that it demands documentation and footnoting support—and assuming the person has done their work to prepare to write the manuscript—I tell them to simply provide a short reference at the time so that they can continue writing now and come back and complete the footnote later. (It is imperative to put in the reference to the primary or secondary source at the time of writing so that it does not get lost. It is amazing how hard it can be to find again that one source that contained such an important fact.) The results of overwriting can often be quite beneficial. Overwriting tends to produce more quickly written and completed manuscripts, and it generates a fair bit of prose that the author can then go back and manipulate into the shape of the final piece.

Verbal Retention

There is a third factor to consider in being a self-critical author, and that is verbal retention. Once words are written—whether it is on a page or on

r screen—they take on a significance and permanence that can
harmful. The prose created by overwriting is often too wordy
y too much of a good thing, but I have noticed that sometimes
difficult for a writer who has produced so much verbiage to be
able simply to delete wording as unnecessary or redundant. Instead, the
tendency is to find a way to recast the passage and still include all the
words. Early on in my writing career, I was doing research into a particular thinker, and there were a number of secondary sources that cited
lists of what he had done. None of the lists matched exactly. In my initial
treatment of this, I wrote down each of the lists. Then, in the course of
revising, I found it very difficult to come up with essentially one list
and to make simple references to other views in a footnote. In the end, I
no doubt included too much because, at the time, I was afraid of losing
something essential. I think that all I did was include too much that was
not of value, and I even ran the risk of diluting the thrust of what I was
trying to say because there was too much verbiage that surrounded it.

In preparing a manuscript for publication, you should be able to examine
the written text and provide an objective assessment of it. One of the keys
to editing your work is to be able to look at each sentence and unit and
answer at least the following questions:

- Do I have a clear thesis statement that is developed throughout
  the written work and that guides every stage of the composition?

- Does this sentence or other unit communicate what I want it to
  communicate, and is this significant enough to merit inclusion in
  this manuscript?

- Does it do so in language that is straightforward and to the
  point?

- Are there too many subordinate clauses, participial clauses, or
  (perish the thought) parenthetical comments that distract from
  the force of what I am saying?

- Is the vocabulary that I have chosen suitable for the intended
  readership and appropriate for the topic?

- Do I provide the kind of support that I need for any point I make,
  whether it is logical or evidential support?

- Do I include enough examples to make clear and illustrate what I am saying?

- Do I allow my prose to breathe; that is, do I develop a rhythm of intensity and relief so as to avoid simply a string of hard-hitting, content-filled statements?

- Do these sentences connect together in a clear and logical sequence that makes sense?

- Is my language idiomatic; for example, do the right prepositions go with the right verbs?

- Do I use the right person (this author, we, I, you, one?) for the occasion?[2]

- Are my paragraphs suitable in length and structure for a manuscript such as this, avoiding both journalistic short paragraphs and swollen, endless paragraphs?

- Do I use appropriate headings at the right intervals to help and enhance my organization?

- Does my introduction get to the main point quickly and clearly?

- Does my conclusion genuinely conclude without introducing new topics not treated?

- When I read through what I have written, does it make sense, without causing me to stumble and get confused over my own writing?

If you can answer positively to all of these questions after reading through and editing your writing, then you are probably on the right track.

One of the inevitable outcomes of submitting manuscripts for possible publication is that you will receive rejection letters from editors and publishers. Rather than being devastated by these letters, which are a part of the process of getting into print, simply learn as much as possible from such experiences. Sometimes you learn enough from incidental comments to provide encouragement for submission to another publisher. At other times, you learn important information that can help in the revision process. There are even occasions when the editor will leave open the possibility of resubmission of a manuscript for a second consideration.

In these cases, knowing how to look at the manuscript and make the appropriate changes can be invaluable. In other words, when rejection letters come, and they will, I encourage you to use them as a further step in getting your manuscript published.

7

Handling Acceptance—It Too Will Come

I am confident that if you follow the guidelines in this book, you will become a published scholarly author. In fact, I am confident that you will be able to develop a publishing research profile that leads from one good publication to another. Because I am so confident that that is the case, I include this chapter. As you can see from what I have said above, even if an article is initially rejected, that should not mean the end of the attempt to get published. Most rejection letters are not a final and definitive "no" but only "not yet," until the piece is revised and submitted again, either to the original publisher or another. So I am confident that virtually every "no" can be turned into not only "not yet" but eventually "yes." However, there is still much work to be done once an author receives one of the much-sought-after letters that says, "Dear Dr. Porter, I am pleased to inform you that. . . ." In this chapter, I want to help you to learn what that work is so that you can expedite it as quickly and efficiently as possible. One of the reasons that I think it is necessary to prepare for acceptance of an article or book—and it will come, I am certain—is so that you can use your time wisely in finishing off this project as you move to the next one. There is nothing quite so conducive to success as success itself. Once you have received one of those acceptance letters, you will want to receive more of those letters and will desire to move on to the next research and writing project as soon as possible. However, an important part of publication is finishing off the projects that have been accepted. The project is finished not with the letter of acceptance but only when the published piece comes out in hard form (or hard electronic form, if there is such a thing). Even then, it may not be finally done if you intend to take that manuscript and use it again in some other publication, such as a collection of essays or a related project.

So what do you do once you have received a letter of acceptance? There are six important topics that I wish to cover in this chapter that will help you through the joys of publishing success: (1) doing what is required, but only what is required; (2) the importance of proofreading; (3) responding to a publisher's requests for additional information; (4) reviews of your work; (5) the preparation of indexes; and (6) some other matters.

Doing What Is Required, but Only What Is Required

When a manuscript is accepted for publication, the editor may send to you any one of a number of different types of acceptance letters. These letters will determine what it is that you are to do next.

Outright Acceptance—Don't Touch a Thing

This type of acceptance letter simply states that your manuscript has been accepted for publication and has been put in the queue for disk cleanup, copyediting, and then the sending of proofs to you in due course. This is very good news, because it means that the publisher has everything that is required of you at this stage—you sent the required hard or soft copies, and they are proceeding with them. At this stage, the last thing that you want to do is to have to contact the publisher and ask her to wait because you have found some material errors in the manuscript, or feel compelled to revise it, or wish to add some late-breaking footnotes. The manuscript that you send to the publisher should be the last and final version of it, and one that you can live with if it were to appear in print in that exact form. After submission—and with it the chance of acceptance for publication—is not the time to have your best "second thoughts" on how to go about writing and presenting your article. Leave well enough alone.

Chance for a Last-Minute Update

Another type of acceptance letter recognizes that, in the period between submission and acceptance, you may have decided to make a few changes. Editors often offer acceptance but then allow you to send the real "final" version of your manuscript. If allowed to do so, and you have some changes to make, then do so quickly and efficiently, but be careful that you do not make too many changes of substance.

Sometimes, however, publications get delayed for various reasons, and as a result an editor may allow you to bring your article up to date after a period of time. I was the editor of a reference volume that was delayed due to some circumstances beyond my control. I communicated with each contributor, offering the chance to bring the manuscript up to date. This update could include any changes in the content of the article, but especially additions to the bibliography, recognizing any recent significant work. I have sent out such notices before, and it is always interesting to see what responses I get. Some basically wrote back and said that their articles were fine and there were no new and significant enough developments to merit change. For some I agreed, but for some others they clearly were not interested in that topic or article any more and chose not to bring it up to date. As their names are on the articles, they will have to bear the brunt of any criticism. For others, it was a chance to tweak some wording here and there, especially if they added bibliography and wanted to include reference to a major new author or work. A final group engaged in massive changes. These often were huge new bibliographies by those who are apparently obsessed with the idea that the only thing of value is the latest and newest thing (the automobile and computer industries certainly count on these people), but there were others who wanted to undertake serious rewriting of their articles. Again, some of this was certainly justified because there had been significant developments in their fields, but others were simply doing the rewriting that they should have done at an earlier stage.

My suggestion is not to count on the opportunity to be able to revise an article later, and so do everything possible to submit the closest to a final version that you can live with. If you are given the chance for revision, be reasonable, and include only significant and major works that will be noticed if they are not there. I don't treat anything I write as necessarily the final thing I will write on a topic, even if I don't have any intention of revisiting a topic, so I always keep open the possibility of a future article that says more about what I think or brings the research up to date.

Subject to Revision

On other occasions, the letter you receive from the editor will say that your manuscript has been accepted, subject to some moderate or modest revisions that the editor is suggesting, and will also offer you a chance to make any other changes. If I receive a letter such as this, I make those changes my first and top priority. I have known authors who take the view that, since the article is accepted, they will get around to the changes when they can. I try to send the required information back the next day or by return e-mail if I am able. I want my part to be done and for the piece to proceed to the next stage as soon as possible, without my delaying it in any way. I want my manuscript out in the next possible fascicle of the journal, not delayed to the next publication year because I chose to take my time in getting around to making required changes. As far as introducing any further changes on my part, as I say above, I try to submit as close to the final product as I can, so that I don't need to do any further work on the manuscript. I recently had this lesson reinforced the hard way when I submitted an article to a publisher. I understood that there was going to be a further stage in which the publisher copyedited the manuscript and then sent to me proofs to correct. Almost immediately after submission of the article, I noticed an error that I had made that required the rewriting of two sentences. I immediately wrote to the editor by e-mail but heard nothing. I followed up a week later only to be told that there was to be no return of the articles to authors for review, and hence no chance to correct at proof stage if the copy editor missed the problem—assuming there is copyediting (I honestly never found out). So I immediately sent my corrections to the editor and instructed that the changes be put in, and received assurances that they would be. The point is that it is easier if you get it right the first time, but if you have to make changes or corrections, do them quickly and as soon as possible.

Not untypically, journals in this day and age often have quite a long backlog of articles to be published. Sometimes this backlog is as long as two to three years before publication. The longest period that I have had to wait is nine years between delivery of the paper at a conference and submission to the editor of the journal soon after, and final publication. This is unusually long, but such things do happen. Sometime during the time of waiting, an author should receive proofs to read before final publication. There is often a temptation on the part of the author to think that because of the delay there need to be some changes and additions made to the article. As an editor, I find such attempts annoying and usually not necessary. As an author, on the one hand, I understand them but realize that, on the other, they often end up having the counterproductive effect of delaying publication further. If significant changes need to be made to an article at this stage, it often means that the entire publication is delayed or, even more likely, that the particular article may be bumped to a later fascicle of the journal. This means further delays and only increases the temptation to desire changes, the start of a vicious and best-avoided cycle.

The secret, I believe, is to do what the editor desires as quickly as possible and either leave the original submission alone or make the changes required by the editor and usually no more. Then, with this finished product in the hands of the editor, the manuscript can proceed to publication as soon as possible.

Proofreading: What It Is and How to Do It

Publishers differ in how much contact they have with authors between acceptance of the manuscript and publication, and this contact also varies according to whether the piece is an article or a book. Often for articles, there is no further communication until proofs arrive—and then the publisher sometimes wants them returned in anything from three to ten days! (No, I am not kidding.) For books, there are often several other stages of communication, possibly even several sets of proofs. If the volume is a jointly written project, such as a collection of essays by different authors, often there are further stages that require coordination of several sets of participants: the individual authors in proofreading, the volume editors in the assemblage of the corrections by the individual contributors, and the publishers. For books, there are often indexes to be prepared as well.

One thing that virtually all publishing projects have in common—the exception being my article mentioned above!—is proofreading.

What Is Proofreading?

Article and book projects require a number of different production stages. In today's publishing process, typically a publisher receives your manuscript in electronic and hard or another permanent form. Once the final manuscript is approved, it goes down one of two paths. Some publishers still send their manuscripts to a copy editor who marks up the copy in terms of both the house style and content. This copy editor may have contact with the author if issues arise, such as a faulty reference, or the need for more information in a note, or simply to clarify sentences that make no sense. The quality of copy editors varies significantly. Some are very knowledgeable and communicate regularly and insightfully, while others simply do their own thing and then send proofs to your inbox. I have worked with some excellent copy editors, and they can be valuable partners in the publishing process. Other publishers do not use copy editors but rely upon authors to do their own copyediting before submission. Once the copyediting is complete—whether it is essentially done by the author or, ideally, by a skilled copy editor—then this copy is given to the so-called "typesetter,"[1] who takes the electronic file and incorporates the copy editor's markings to produce a set of proofs.

Some publishers switch the procedures above and initially give the electronic file to a person to conform the manuscript to the guidelines of the publisher. Sometimes this is called disk cleanup. The person doing this may or may not be an editor. If the person is not, then the cleaned-up file, which generally conforms to the parameters of the publisher, may go to a copy editor. More and more, with all of the production being outsourced by publishers, the person doing disk cleanup and the copy editor are the same person, and the entire task is performed in a single step using the electronic file.

Nevertheless, through one means or another, eventually such things as proofs are produced. In days past, first when type was set by hand and then when it was set mechanically by linotype machines, this process gave a chance to test what had been set. Now the term "proofs" persists, and the function of checking is still there, but proofs are not a means of authenticating set type but of checking for editing and authorial errors. These proofs are referred to in various ways by different publishers. Some give names to the proofs—such as author's proofs, line proofs (where there are lines on the pages to show page parameters, etc.), final proofs, etc. Others give numbers to the proofs—first proofs (usually internally proofread), second proofs (usually corrected proofs that go to the author), etc., with as many numbered proofs as necessary or feasible before being printed. Most publishers understandably prefer to keep their number of proofs to a minimum.

As an author, you do not need to be concerned with the numbering or naming of the proofs. All you need to be concerned with is reading the proofs that you are sent, correcting them as quickly and efficiently as you are able, and returning them to the publisher so that the piece can be published. In today's publishing context, sometimes the proofs will only come to you electronically, usually as a pdf, occasionally with line numbering; sometimes the proofs will come to you in hard form. In either case, you need to agree with the publisher on a form of conveying back to the publisher what the results of your proofreading are in terms of corrections, changes, and alterations. As noted above, I would resist strong temptations to make any significant changes at the proof stage.[2] It may be that you discover a word that is used redundantly, or an awkward phrase that can be conveniently corrected. I would definitely make such changes but avoid any wholesale rewriting.

Publishers often like to scare authors by stating that they will charge for unnecessary corrections. The reality is that publishers often threaten to make such charges but rarely do so. Nevertheless, this does not mean that I would want to tempt them to charge me for any changes. Besides, putting in new material means increasing the chance that new errors will be introduced into the proof.

How to Proofread

Proofreading is a greater challenge for an author than is often realized. Authors often assume that the publisher has gone through the piece meticulously, and after all, the person at the publishing house is a professional, so there is nothing more for the author to do. In many instances, this is the case. However, project managers (as they are better called, as editing does not describe fully what they do) are increasingly being asked to do so many things—disk cleanup, layout, copyediting, proofreading, and final production—that it is impossible to believe that one person can always get everything exactly right. What I have noticed with many academic publishers is that the editors they are using are excellent at the mechanical part of the task. They know the house style very well and can apply it to a document. They know how to manipulate the technical details so that pagination is good, no widows or orphans are on the pages, and the footnotes generally follow the correct format. However, they usually are not subject specialists, and they do not read the text of the articles well or with understanding and insight, and sometimes do not pick up some of the finer points of technical details regarding a particular discipline (e.g., how certain primary sources are cited). As a result, there are a number of content problems that slip through. These are not egregious errors—which authors and editors should have caught before submission—but the kinds of things that publishers and editors in the past would probably have corrected. This makes the task of proofreading all the more necessary.

Authors must realize that, while it is certainly true that the publisher's name is on the book or the journal's title is on the article, the ultimate responsibility for a published piece—including both its technical presentation and the content—rests with the author. The author is the one whose reputation goes up or down depending on the number of typographical errors and the other problems that can accompany publication. It is the author's responsibility to ensure that these are eliminated. Certainly careful preparation of the manuscript at all its stages—research, writing, and submission—is essential to ensuring error-free work. Proofreading is the last chance that an author has to make sure that this is done well.

As mentioned above, proofs come either electronically or in hard form. I would seriously and strongly suggest that, even if they come in electronic form, you print out the proofs and correct the hard copy. As I mentioned previously, I believe that most authors are much better at proofreading with pen and paper than on-screen. It takes quite a bit of regular and repeated practice for a proofreader to become as good proofreading on-screen as on hard copy. This difficulty is doubly compounded when the author is expected to proofread his or her own material. The possibility for missing mistakes goes up dramatically.

The task of proofreading is to go through the publication to check every detail to ensure its accuracy. At this stage, this process does not include checking the accuracy of quotations or page references in secondary sources, as these should have been caught in advance. However, at proof stage, editors may well include queries to the author where a detail or reference is needed or needs to be checked. These queries should be responded to as quickly and efficiently as possible as part of the proofreading task. The major issue in proofreading, however, is to verify the text and layout of the piece. The primary task is to read the text to ensure that every matter of a technical sort concerning the text is accurate. This usually does not mean checking larger layout matters. Instead, it requires checking issues such as spelling, punctuation, capitalization, indentation, headers or footers on the page, headings and their levels and styles, pagination of the proofs, and the like. One of the challenges is that the manuscript is now set according to the house style of the publisher and so may look radically different from what you submitted or are used to. As the author, you must read the proofs in the light of the house style of the publisher—even though you may not know that house style particularly well. In some instances, this means that you may need to query the editor back to ensure that a particular way that something is done conforms to the house style. To check against, you should always have in front of you when proofreading a copy of the final version of the manuscript that was submitted to the publisher.

The natural tendency is for authors to read proofs from start to finish (I suggest a refinement on this method below). This is certainly one way of doing it, and it has an inherent logic to it. As you read, you check all matters. An article consists of essentially one proofreadable item—the article consisting of the title, author's name (and possibly institution or place), and then the article itself. A book can be divided into two parts at this stage. The first part is the preliminary material, and the second is the content of the book. A book is clearly more complicated to proofread than an article, because there is more substance and complexity to it.

For an article, rather than simply diving into the body of the piece, you should begin your proofreading by checking the title of the article and then the information about the author (is your name spelled correctly and the way that you always have it on your publications?) and academic affiliation. Then you should turn to the article itself. If there are headings, they should be checked to be sure they are continuously numbered or lettered and in the appropriate style for each level. The content needs to be checked carefully, including spelling, punctuation, and the like. A common problem is to figure out the principles used for punctuation with quotations, especially those publications using British standards. Footnotes or endnotes need to be carefully checked as well to be sure that the spelling, punctuation, and style are correct and consistent throughout.

For a book, you begin by checking the preliminary pages. These pages include the title page, bibliographical information page, table of contents, preface, foreword, acknowledgments, abbreviations, list of tables or illustrations, and anything else that might be included. If any of these items have information repeated elsewhere in the book, such as titles of chapters in the contents and on the first page of a new chapter, they should be checked to ensure they match. If they are available, you should also check the back material, such as indexes, to ensure accuracy (I had one book appear in which my own name was misspelled in the index—but I was not given the opportunity to proofread the indexes). Then you turn to the content of the book. As with an article, you need to check the chapter headings and any other headings for enumeration and style; the footnotes or endnotes; and the spelling, punctuation, and style of the content of the chapter.

There are, of course, peculiarities that distinguish each publisher. I have mentioned a number of these in discussing guidelines for submitting potential manuscripts for publication. Some of these distinctions only become obvious when you receive proofs and notice that some elements of your manuscript have been changed. These peculiarities include the spelling and punctuation conventions followed, the style for footnotes, and the references to sources, among others. A few of the others to note that are easy to miss are whether the publisher uses a hyphen (-), en dash (–), or em dash (—), and where. For example, some publishers use a hyphen for page numbers and an en dash for years, thus pp. 17-19 and 1985–1987, while others use an en dash for all numbers. The em dash is usually used for the dash that is found in parenthetical material, but this is not always the case, and some use it to separate larger numerical units. Observing such fine points will distinguish the careful from the not-so-careful proofreader.

Despite all of the care that you will take with proofreading, it is easy to miss various mistakes. Major reasons for missing these items are, first of all, that this is your own material, and so you know what it is supposed to say and how it is supposed to say it. Hence, you will tend to read it this way in the proofs, with or without mistakes. Another reason is that you may be expert in a number of areas without having developed the skills necessary for proofreading—otherwise perhaps you would be a proof-reader. One way of overcoming these difficulties is to have someone else read your proofs for you. The advantage of this is that the person did not write the article or book and so does not know what it is supposed to say. They need to read it for accuracy without necessarily reading that accuracy into it. The difficulty here is that there is no guarantee that another person can do the proofreading any better than you can—unless you hire a professional proofreader. There may be an occasion when that is advisable or good to do; however, I don't think that you necessarily need to if you follow the guidelines that I am giving here and take care and time with the proofreading task.

One of the common recurring problems with proofreading is the fact that the author knows what the proofs are supposed to say. Even an outside proofreader will be able to guess what comes next on the basis of knowing the language (knowledge of the language should be, I think, a necessary minimal requirement for proofreading). I have found that one of the best ways of overcoming this difficulty is to proofread *backward*, that is, to proofread from back to front of the document, reading each word one at a time, beginning with the last word and going forward to the first word. For you novices to proofreading, I actually suggest that you proofread twice, as well as possibly having a trusted, informed, and educated friend or colleague proofread. The first time through the proofs I suggest that you proofread backward, and the second time frontward. The benefits of proofreading backward are numerous. You must pay attention to every word, because each word occurs individually. As a result, you must examine and check the spelling of every word. This will not necessarily help with homophones, such as "there" and "their," except that in such cases you should then read the sentence to ensure the proper form is being used. Going back to front also makes you pay attention to other details that might be missed or gone over too quickly. These might include ensuring that a capital letter comes before a period or full stop (as you read backward), or that the punctuation is inside or outside the quotation marks as appropriate. Reading backward is simply a more time-consuming task, and so it forces you to take longer to look at each word, symbol, or element. I know that this may seem like an awfully tedious process—and who, you may ask, does this anyway? Well, I used to do this for every article that I proofread, until I trained my eye to pay attention to as much detail as was needed to be able to proofread well.

The key to good proofreading is to do a thorough, accurate, and timely job in reading proofs and to get the corrections back to the publisher as soon as possible in a clear and concise way.

How to Communicate Changes to the Editor

A whole set of conventions has been developed for communicating the changes that are to be made in proofs—the so-called proofreader's marks. These marks have been made less necessary by those publishers who send proofs electronically, because these publishers usually want the author to send back corrections in an electronic form. I will discuss the way to do that below. However, it is wise to learn the standard proofreader's marks anyway, because they form a very convenient shorthand to use in marking the proof that you print out from the electronic file and in conveying this information back to the publisher. The usefulness of this set of conventions was made apparent to me in a very obvious way when

I received my proofs from a publisher for a book where the typesetter clearly did not know well either of the major languages used throughout the volume (one modern and the other ancient). My proofreading of the ancient language sometimes identified as many as five to seven corrections per line. The necessary corrections could be conveniently marked because of the system of proofreader's marks. These symbols indicate both the type of correction to be made and a means for organizing these corrections by putting a corresponding unique mark at the appropriate place in the text and in the margin for each correction. For example, let's say that (in the unusual circumstance) you want to insert individual words at several places in a single line. At the first place where you wish to insert a word, you might indicate the insertion by using an insert mark, ⟨, both at the place in the line where the word is to be added and in the margin where you write the word. In both the line of text and the margin where you wish to add the second word, you might use a virgule with a crossbar, ⌐; the third might be a virgule with two crossbars, ⊏; the fourth might be a virgule with a small round circle on the top, ℘; and the next a virgule with a small round circle on the bottom, ∂, etc. In other words, one simply needs to match the mark in the text with the correction in the margin in order to correct the proofs.

The major proofreader's marks can be fairly easily identified. Each publisher has their own version of these marks, but they are consistent enough from one to the other that I have never had any trouble using the ones that I am familiar with to communicate with the publisher. Many publishers like these marks to be put in a colored ink, such as red or green. Sometimes publishers send out proofs that have the proofreader's marks of other readers on them, such as an internal proofreader, and so they like the author to use a different-colored ink in order to identify the person making the correction. One of the most important concepts to keep in mind is that for every indication in the text, there should be a corresponding indication in the margin with a correction to guide the typesetter.

Here is a brief and admittedly incomplete guide to proofreader's marks to help you learn to recognize and use such marks:

Marginal Mark	*Textual Mark*	*Meaning*
⋏	⋏	Insertion. This can indicate an insertion between words, or substitution of what is written in the margin for what is already in the text, whether it is a letter or a larger unit of material.
∧ or #	⋏	Insert space, e.g., a letter space between words or between letters.
℘	/ or ⊢	Delete a letter with the virgule or delete all of the letters or words that are lined through from the first to the second vertical line.
⌣	⌣	Close up space between letters or words.
℘	⌣	Delete letter and close up.
∽	∽	Transpose items within the enclosed areas.
>--------		Put more space between lines.
(--------		Leave less space between lines.
□	□	Start new line.
↵	↵	Run on one line to another.
⌐	⌐	Indent.
⌐	⌐	Do not indent.
¶	⋏	Start new paragraph.

The following marginal marks should be put in a circle:

Marginal Mark	Textual Mark	Meaning
. or , or ; or :	$\wedge$	Insert punctuation as indicated
' or '	$\vee$	Insert opening or closing quotation mark or apostrophe
caps	$\equiv$ under letters	Change to capital letters
lc	/	Change to lowercase letters
sc	= under letters	Change to small capital letters
rom	circle letters	Change to nonitalic (roman) font
ital	underline letters	Change to italicized font
bf	$\approx$ under letters	Change to bold font
wf	circle letters	Wrong font
sp	circle letters	Spell out the abbreviation
stet	. . . . under letters	Leave as printed, i.e., do not change
run on	line connecting text	Run on one line to another
close up	(space)	Remove a line or more of space

If you have not marked proofs before, it will take some time to get used to doing it. The important factor is to make your corrections as clear as you can by using the symbols above. There are other symbols as well, and often publishers will send you a brief sheet that outlines the symbols that they prefer. If there is any doubt in your mind whether what you have indicated is clear, you can always write the typesetter a note (assuming you are sending back physical proofs). One of the standard rules in publishing is that material written in the margin is to be inserted into the text, but material written and circled is meant as a note to the typesetter. Thus, if there is something that you think is potentially ambiguous or problematic, do not hesitate to write the typesetter or editor a note. In the note, you may even wish to write out what the final product should look like. The key is to be sure that you circle this material so that your note does not end up being put into the text by accident. (A good editor will catch such a thing, but you don't want to find out that your editor was napping as your proofs came through.)

If you have received hard copy proofs, then you should probably send them back in hard copy or, if time is of the essence, fax them back. I always make a photocopy before I return corrected proofs so that, if anything happens, I do not have to read the proofs again. Sometimes proofs can get lost in the mail, or the editor wants to follow up one of my corrections and needs for me to look at my proofs to decipher a cryptic comment. If I have a photocopy of the corrected proofs, I can look at them to decipher my symbols, rather than trying to remember what I must have said.

If your proofs have come electronically, you have several choices on how to send corrections back, besides sending back the corrected printed-out copy of the proofs. Some editors want you to make corrections on the pdf, if you have that capability. That is not the preferred means of correcting proofs, as it requires you to have a more advanced computer program, and it makes it more difficult to trace the corrections. A more likely alternative is that the editor wants you to read the proofs and then send back by e-mail the set of corrections. When you do that, there is no set means of communicating the information. Again, the key is to be as clear as possible. If proofs are not particularly clean and require significant editing, writing out all of the changes can be quite tiresome, and it leaves open the distinct possibility of introducing new errors. What I try to provide, when I send back electronic corrections, is as clear a description of what I am correcting as is possible. For example, I treat each page as a unit and then break it down by paragraphs and lines. I count the first paragraph on the page, even if incomplete because it begins on the previous page, as number one. Lines are from the top of the page or paragraph unless otherwise indicated. I also usually give the correct reading, then indicate the reading that is being replaced, and then sometimes describe what the change is. Thus, I might write something like the following:

> p. 17 par. 1 line 17 [= page 17, paragraph 1, line 17 from the top of that paragraph], read: he elucidated the points (not he elucadates, correcting spelling and tense)

> p. 22 par. 2 line 3 from bottom, read: was she seen, before (not she was seen before, changing word order and adding comma)

> p. 33 first indented quotation line 3, read: cats. The (capitalize The)

Some authors go back and check their corrected proofs against the published article once it is published. If you have kept a corrected copy, you can do that. As I rarely go back and read straight through anything I have published before, I cannot say that I remember ever going back and deliberately checking the corrections. After all, once the article is in print, there is nothing I can do about it—and there certainly is no point in fretting about it. Remember the story of the scholar who realized that two of the pages had been reversed in his article? If he had not gone back and checked the article, he never would have known, and he would not have had to dread the embarrassment of discovery that never occurred. He feared that his scholarly reputation would be in tatters, because people would not be able to make sense of his argument due to the transposed pages, and, as the author of the piece, this would reflect badly upon him and his scholarship. Needless to say, no one ever noticed—or at least no one ever told him or mentioned in print that the pages had been switched.

Responding to a Publisher's Requests for Additional Information

While the article or book is in the process of being set up for publication, including the sending out of proofs, at some stage the publisher will probably send to you a set of communications requesting further information.

Contract

The first such communication may well be a contract. I repeat here what I said above, that I am not a lawyer, so I cannot and will not give legal advice. What I will mention is what I have encountered. For an article, this communication might involve a small contract that turns over copyright to the publisher in return for publishing your article. Some authors choose to retain copyright of all of their work, while others gladly sign it over, letting the publisher worry if someone else wants to use or reprint the article. The key here is that publishers should allow authors to have access to their own work to reuse, for example, in collections of essays or in other forms. Good ones do. I would encourage you to publish with those who gladly welcome the further dissemination—of course, giving appropriate credit to them—of their authors' work.

The contract for a book is more complex, and you may wish to get a lawyer to look at the book contract before you sign it. In my experience, most publishing contracts are pretty standard legal boilerplate, and since for the kinds of books that I am talking about here—scholarly works of serious merit, not the kind of pop stuff that goes into the popular book stores and trade sales—the money at stake for the author is fairly minimal, worrying about movie rights and other such things is probably not going to be worth much time and effort.

There are, however, two typical clauses included in contracts that every author needs to be aware of. I have become aware of these clauses through reading and signing numerous contracts and believe that you need to be aware of them and think through their implications.[3]

The first is the clause concerning the "second book option." A number of publishers include in their contracts a standard clause stating that they obligate you to give them the right of first refusal on your second or subsequent volume. Some authors appreciate this clause because they believe that it indicates that someone desires their written work. However, this is just an inexpensive way of ensuring that the publisher does not have to look for books but has them delivered anyway. I would suggest that you consider getting this clause taken out of the contract. Many publishers know that this inhibits your ability to choose to market a book wherever you may wish, and causes undue publication delays as the publisher examines a manuscript that they may not even have a category for. If you submit such a manuscript, don't be surprised if it is rejected. Most reasonable publishers will understand if you wish to scratch such a clause out. Slightly more problematic is the second clause, the "noncompetition clause," that some publishers include in their contracts. This clause basically states that while the contracted work is in print you agree not to enter into competition with another publisher by publishing a similar work. This sounds reasonable, until you explore what it means to publish a similar work. How close is similar? At this point, the implications of such a clause become problematic. I think that it is best either to consider having such a clause removed from the contract or to get the publisher to agree to wording that makes it very specific what constitutes a similar work. This should basically mean not a work in the same general field, but a work that is identical to the one you are publishing. Publishers who wish to keep authors happy and publishing with them should be able to agree to this.

There are other communications, however, that authors will receive in the course of publishing their manuscripts. Most of them are less potentially problematic than the contract. Most of these matters are also specifically related to the publishing of books, whether as author or editor. These include the author questionnaire, the list of review journals, cover blurbs, endorsements, and other cover and advertising material.

Author Questionnaire

The author questionnaire is the most important of these remaining communication items—and, if you have published very much, often the most frustrating. I have now published multiple books with several different publishers, and they still send me an author questionnaire for each book. I guess they are worried that I have changed my name or address or birth date since the last time I filled the form out for them. Publishers are notoriously inefficient in some of these areas of information retention and retrieval. I have had the very frustrating occasion of providing for a publisher a list of contact information for contributors to a given book three times, and still being asked for the list by another editor. One editor takes and puts it in the book file, another sends it to the project manager handling the book, and another one must use it for a napkin while eating lunch. In any case, some of this material gets provided on numerous occasions, sometimes for the same book, so it is wise to keep this standard information on your computer so that it can be sent again at a moment's notice.

Some of the other information requested on the questionnaire is genuinely unique to the book, such as the length and type of book (yes, you still have to fill this out even if they already have the book manuscript in their hands and could easily check it themselves), the potential audience, places the book might be advertised and sold, a short description for advertising purposes or for an inside flap of a dust jacket, a longer description for the back cover or for a longer advertising flyer, and the like. The questionnaire often includes suggestions for marketing the book, such as conferences for the publisher to attend at which to promote the book or societies that might have members who would be interested. Occasionally, in my experience, publishers pay attention to such ideas, but most have their designated conferences that they attend and the standard means of advertising. There are also usually a number of unique questions that a particular publisher wants to ask.

Reviewing Journals

Another piece of communication concerns the list of potential reviewing journals. Most publishers have a master list that includes a small set of journals that this particular publisher always sends books to. The rest of the choices are often up to you as the author. The publisher usually has a limit on the number of review copies that will be sent out. In traditional publishing, the review copies often come out of what is sometimes called the overrun, that is, the number of books that the printer actually prints beyond the number ordered by the publisher. So in a run of 1,000 books, the publisher might actually receive 1,037 copies of the book. This takes care of the author's free copies and review copies and leaves 1,000 to sell. In other words, the author's copies and review copies rarely cost the publisher anything, despite their vehement protests when you ask for a couple more gratis copies. In the age of print-on-demand publishing, there is no overrun, as the printer only prints the number ordered. If the publisher puts in an order for twelve books, twelve will get printed, so there are not as many review copies potentially available, because each one actually costs the publisher money to produce.

There are several keys to selecting the journals for review of a book. The first and most important is to be sure that the journal actually reviews books and doesn't just have a list of books received in the back. There are a number of very prestigious journals in most disciplines that do not review books. Yet they are sent a large number of books, simply on the basis of their reputation. On occasion these journals print a list of books received in the back, but being listed here is not the same as getting a review. Where do you think all of those books go? Does the conscientious journal editor return them to the publisher? Probably not. They go on the shelf of the editor, or to his graduate students, or even to a used book dealer. That is one of the hazards of sending books out for review—

oftentimes they won't be reviewed. It behooves the author to be sure that, with a finite number of review copies available, those copies get into the hands of those who actually review books—though there can be no guarantee that a book will be reviewed. A second factor to keep in mind is that you probably want to get your book distributed to as wide a range of types of journals as possible. There is no point in sending the book only to one type of journal. The reason for this is that a review in one journal within a subsection of a discipline is probably enough to establish the reputation of the book. More reviews in the same subset simply mean that the same people of the same perspective are reading more reviews. If the book is reviewed in a variety of types of journals, then the book has a better chance of wider dissemination and influence.

Cover and Advertising Material

If a request for copy for the cover is not included in the author questionnaire, the publisher may well ask you later for blurbs for advertising and for cover use. Some publishers write these blurbs themselves, but many ask the author to do it, as the author knows the content of the book best. However, publishers are usually wise enough to edit these cover blurbs, because the authors of academic books are notoriously poor at writing forceful and hard-hitting advertising copy—and that is what the material on the book cover is all about. The material on the cover should give a straightforward and appealing description of the major thrust of the book, especially indicating major features that should excite interest within the field. The author is usually also asked to provide a description of himself or herself. This is meant to be brief and to the point. It usually covers such information as name—it is important, I believe, to use the same name for all your publications, so that people are not confused as to whether you or someone else with a similar name is writing the latest publication—degrees held and often place received, current academic appointment including rank and institution, and sometimes former institutions, especially if they are worth mentioning. Publishers are often ambivalent about authors listing previous publications, unless they are with that particular publisher. Some publishers list their names along with the titles of books they have published, but give only the titles of books published by other companies.

The fad today is for publishers to have other scholars write endorsements for books that they publish. This is one of the greatest acts of bravado in the publishing business, because some of the authors I know who have been asked to write such blurbs do not actually bother or are not able to read the manuscript with appropriate carefulness before writing the endorsement. One of the reasons for this is that publishers often only ask scholars to comment on a book late in the game and just before going to print. As an author, you will often be asked to suggest names of people who may write such endorsements. Publishers also often have their stable of people who will write such endorsements on demand according to subject. I recommend suggesting names of people you think may well be favorable toward what you are doing, rather than naming one of the people you take on head to head in your monograph. The safety factor is that the publishers have the choice of not using an endorsement that is not positive—although there are some that sometimes slip through that are less than stellar in their endorsement—and they certainly can edit the statement if they need to.

If you as an author are asked for an endorsement of a book, I would suggest that you accept, because it means you will be given a free copy of the book once it is published. I would also suggest that you say positive things if you believe that you can endorse the book, and not send an endorsement if you think that you cannot. (I would also suggest agreeing in advance with the editor who contacts you that you receive a copy of the book when published regardless of whether you endorse it or whether your endorsement is used, just so you get something for your effort.) One thing that I would not do is list the endorsements that you have given in your curriculum vitae (c.v.) as if they are published works. I know that there are some scholars who appear to have made their primary means of scholarly publication the endorsement or foreword, and some might even publish their collected prefaces, forewords, and endorsements some day (I do not recommend this approach to publication). The saving grace in all of this business over endorsements, however, is that they should not be taken seriously at all, and are not by most informed people. For you as a scholar, no one should be influencing whether you buy, read, or accept the argument of a book simply because some scholar with a big name (or a propensity for endorsing and blurbing every book that comes along) has said that this is the greatest one since, well, since the last one he blurbed. I pay little attention to blurbs and in fact have often found myself turned off by a book simply because of the people who have endorsed it. In other words, you can write an excellent scholarly work that will make a contribution and endure without having to get the approval of Scholar Know-It-All on the back cover.

There may be other material that a publisher requires as well. The key is simply to give as much to them as they need in order to help them to publish and sell your book.

Reviews of Your Work

One of the anticipated results of publishing is to have your book reviewed in the scholarly journals by your peers. I am not going to offer here a critique of the entire reviewing process, but I think that there are a couple of features of the process that should be clarified as you make your way forward in the world of publishing.

The first important observation is that you probably will receive some good and some not-so-good reviews. A written piece of substantial scholarship will almost inevitably arouse such a response. If it does not, it may say something about the scholarship rather than the reviewers. A major reason for this kind of mixed response is that serious and significant scholarship must, or at least should, by definition, challenge received traditions and assured results, and this is bound to arouse the approbation of some scholars who are similarly pushing the boundaries, and the opprobrium of scholars who like the status quo just fine as it is. As a result, a scholar cannot take reviews too seriously. Of course, the good reviews should be enjoyed, pinned up on office walls, photocopied, and distributed to students and friends, but even these should be taken with a grain of salt. Bad reviews should of course be vilified, their authors' characters impugned, and the journals in which the reviews appear castigated with vows never to publish anything with them ever, and indubitably whatever is said taken with a grain of salt.

In truth, both good and bad reviews should be read for what you can gain from them. If a reviewer, whether ultimately positive or negative, makes a significant point about the structure, argumentation, content, or perspective of one of my books, I want to be able to take the comment on its own merits, weigh it against what I think and know about the book, and learn where it is appropriate so that I can make corrections in a subsequent edition or learn to do something in a better way for future research. The rest of it—good and bad—can be and should be easily sloughed off. I realize that those who review books are the same people whom I sit next to in my office, who have the same problems as I do, the same constraints on time, the same insecurities, and all the rest, and so they are susceptible to all the limitations of other human endeavors. Sometimes they get it right and sometimes they don't. Rarely does anyone get it all one way or the other.

In some cases, a particularly lengthy or negative review may merit a response by you as the author. However, you certainly do not want to become saddled with a reputation for going after every negative reviewer. The reviewers get tired of it, and the editors get even more tired of it. I know of an instance where a book was negatively reviewed by a person who has a reputation for being very fair and evenhanded. The author of the book was given a chance to respond to the review and challenged whether the reviewer really knew how to review books. The reviewer, who was in fact a very experienced reviewer and journal editor, was given a last chance to respond. That was not sufficient for the author, who "demanded" another exchange, which was appropriately denied. At the end of the day, the one who comes off looking bad is the original author, certainly not the temperate reviewer.

A question that sometimes arises is whether an author can or should try to influence reviews. By that, I do not mean suggesting that your publisher send out every review copy of the book with a check for $100 or a gift certificate—as a reviewer, I think that that would be very nice, though probably slightly problematic (make the gift small, unmarked bills, and we'll see what we can do). What I mean is the gray areas of whether you help to choose reviewers by suggesting names to publishers, whether you ensure that certain people are sent review copies, or whether you should have contact with those who you know are reviewing your book. It is almost inevitable in many if not most academic disciplines that those who are specialists in a field will know a good number of the other specialists, and so it is virtually impossible not to know who is reviewing someone else's work. However, having known that, I have usually consciously stayed away from the topic of my own work if I have met or spoken with someone who is reviewing one of my books, even if the person is a friend. On one occasion I took an unusual approach, when a negative review of one of my books appeared and a year or so later I inadvertently met the editor of the journal. We had a very pleasant conversation, during which time I realized that for various reasons the editor shared my perspective on a number of scholarly topics. At the end of our conversation, I mentioned to him that I had enjoyed our conversation but was disappointed that his journal had given my book an uncompliment-ary review. He was not aware of the review and said he would look it up. That was the last of our conversation, but a number of months later I noticed that my book was reviewed a second time by that journal, this time by the editor himself, and it was given a much more positive review. Was this inappropriate behavior on my part? I do not think so, as my conversation with the editor was not instigated or carried out with the idea of influencing his opinion or getting a second review. All of that was of his doing. I do believe, however, that it was within my rights to inquire regarding the initial negative review. If he on further thought wished to moderate the first review, that was his decision—and a very wise and insightful one, I might add as well!

Preparation of Indexes

Indexes can be tedious and time consuming to prepare but are essential for scholarly books. When I began in publishing, indexes for books were still usually prepared from proofs by means of index cards. This was the case if you were an author preparing your own indexes, and certainly true if you worked in a publishing house and had to prepare someone else's indexes. That has all changed now, so that there are a number of computer programs available whereby the author can indicate items in the text and the program can prepare the index. While this is available, this is not the procedure I recommend for indexing. I will outline the method I recommend below. After all, unless you wish to pay a fee to the publisher, indexes are the responsibility of the author.

The first consideration for preparing indexes is to decide what kind and type of indexes you wish to include. Your publisher may have some-thing to say about this, on the basis of their preferences. Sometimes the publisher prescribes the type of index or indexes to be included, while other times the author alone suggests the types of indexes. Some books have what is called a consolidated index. This consolidated index includes everything to be indexed within the one index—such as subjects and topics, key ideas and concepts, modern authors, and the like. These are usually not very helpful indexes. There are also specific types of indexes. These include indexes of modern authors cited within the work, indexes of subjects and topics treated in the volume, and, sometimes, depending on the subject matter, indexes of primary and often ancient sources. The subject or topic index is by far the most difficult to prepare, because it requires more discretionary judgment in devising, whereas the others are more referential in nature and hence straightforward.

Most publishers expect the author to prepare the indexes. I often think that the quality of the indexing is an indication of the care that the author has taken in preparing a given book. In the early stages of your publishing career, I would recommend that you take responsibility for your indexes, instead of unloading them on a secretary or a graduate assistant. Such a person may be able to prepare a first draft of the index, but there are often fine points for presentation of indexes that can be tricky, and the author often needs to ensure that these guidelines are followed. Further, an author often learns through the indexing process, such as by recognizing inconsistencies in citation methods or gaining awareness regarding use of sources. As a result, I recommend that authors on most occasions prepare their own indexes, and the way that I suggest below is an efficient means to completing them.

I use a procedure I learned from a good friend, by which it is possible to create up to three indexes at a time with one pass through the manuscript. These indexes should be created from the final proofs, just before the book is published, to ensure that the final pagination is set. There are few more niggling tasks to perform than going through a book after it has been indexed to adjust the index to reflect late changes in pagination. Authors should try to avoid this at all costs. When using a book, I sometimes come across index references that are a page off. Not only is this frustrating, but it indicates that there was probably a late shift in pagination of the book that was not caught by the publisher. A clear advantage of preparing your own indexes is that it gives you a last chance to go through the manuscript and catch any last errors and especially any internal inconsistencies that may have been missed. Such inconsistencies might include how primary and secondary sources are cited, the spelling of names of authors, and other incidental facts and references. For example, I have been able to bring into consistent reference form whether an author is cited by a first name or initials, or how many initials, and on other occasions found that the name of a scholar was misspelled, because my index came up with two spellings for one name.

The tools that you need to index a book are only two: the final proofs of the manuscript and a computer. I have the manuscript to my left on the desk and then open on my computer desktop the number of files that I need for the required indexes. In my areas of research, I usually do two indexes at the same time, but it is possible to do three. I configure the open files so that they do not overlap but are open side by side on the screen. They will consequently be vertically oriented, which is appropriate for an index list to be sent to a publisher. I title the files and save them so that they can continue to record saved information. I also set the margins, columns, and tabs for the indexes. I usually have the regular page parameters in place but have the page set for two columns on a page. I then set two different types of tabs. For indexes of modern authors and subjects, I don't need any particular tabs, because after every name or subject entry I simply enter two spaces and then the page on which the entry appears. For indexes of ancient sources, which I often create, I set a tab far enough to the right so that I can make the entry, tab, and then insert the page number. Of course, if I am simply doing a single consolidated index, I may choose to do several passes through each page of the manuscript as I outline below, but the information will all be entered in only a single file.

I am now ready to begin indexing. Indexes do not include material found in the preliminary material, such as the title page, table of contents, foreword, or preface. The first page to index is usually the introduction or first chapter. Let's say that I will start with the modern author index (and I usually include editors, to aid in finding collected works). I activate this file on my desktop so that my cursor is in the correct place to input the names of authors. I then scan down the first page to be indexed, and every time I note a modern author I enter his or her name in my list: last name first; then a comma, a space, and the first name; then two spaces and the page number. I then hit the return to be ready for the next entry. It is often the case that authors referred to in the body text only have their last names listed, so I have to check the footnotes to get the first names or initials. I continue to do this all the way down the page until I am done. I index all modern authors on the page. If I see that the author is cited more than once, I will only enter it once, but if I enter it more than that it is no problem, as I will show below. Besides authors proper, I enter editors of volumes right alongside, to facilitate finding secondary sources. I then activate the save function to save what I have entered on that monograph page.

Once I am done with that particular page for modern authors and editors, I activate the file of subjects or topics and scan the same page for these entries. As I have stated above, the subject index is more difficult, because trying to define a subject, where it begins and ends, and its subareas involves many judgment calls. The tendency is to be too broad in the categories, rather than more specific. The broader the category, the less useful the entry is. If a monograph is on social construct theory, and this topic is mentioned on most pages, there probably should not be an entry in the index with "Social Construct Theory passim" or "1–293," "295–386," as such an entry is next to worthless. Instead, the various subareas within social construct theory would be more appropriate. Any topic is too large if it is the same size as a chapter. The general topic of the book and the titles of the individual chapters are retrievable from the title of the book and the table of contents, so an index is not needed to find this information. Instead, areas treated within a chapter should be indexed. As with the modern authors, the indexer enters the word or two for the topic, puts in two spaces, and then enters the page number. After saving, I go to the last index.

For the final index of my book, I wish to list ancient sources (this works for any primary textual sources). Again, I scan the page to be indexed—now being scanned for the third time—and note every ancient source and record the page. Ancient sources have some peculiarities with regard to how much information should be included, whether abbreviations of titles of ancient works should be used, in some cases whether Latin or English titles are used, and the like. In any case, if this book is treating ancient Greek tragedy, an ancient source might be Aeschylus's play *The Agamemnon*, lines 117–19. The indexer would enter Aeschylus, Ag. (if abbreviations are permitted) 117–19, then tab over to the set distance and enter the page number. The indexer must also remember that with ancient sources it might be necessary to italicize the titles of works, which can be done at the consolidation stage (e.g., Ag. would then be italicized to *Ag.*).

With the page done, the indexer is now ready to go to the next page, until the entire set of index lists is completed. Along the way, as I note above, the indexer may discover inconsistencies in the manuscript. This is the last time to note these, and they should be corrected.

Once the three complete index lists are done, the indexer's job is not finished, however. The indexer needs to order and consolidate the individual lists into one consistent list for each index. The modern author index is the easiest in this regard. The indexer should use the sort function to place the authors into one continuous alphabetical list from A to

Z. Some computers with smaller capacity may require that the sorting task be broken down into several smaller sorts that are later consolidated in a final sort. In any case, once the list is alphabetized, consolidation begins. The indexer must combine all of the references to a given author —be sure that it is actually the same author and not another with the same last name. The page numbers need to be consolidated also. Publishers have different standards for pagination, but my general rule is to list individually one or two pages but then connect together three or more. So an entry for an author might read this way after sorting and before consolidation:

Johnson, Paul 3

Johnson, Paul 4

Johnson, Paul 6

Johnson, Paul 7

Johnson, Paul 8

Johnson, Paul 9

Johnson, Paul 27

Johnson, Paul 28

Johnson, Paul 29

Johnson, Paul 30

Johnson, Paul 31

Johnson, Paul 32

Johnson, Paul 33

Johnson, Paul 34

Johnson, Paul 35

The entry after consolidation would look like this:

Johnson, Paul 3, 4, 6–9, 27–35

This entry includes every page on which the author is mentioned. There is usually no reason to have "f." or "ff." in an index, but the precise pages should be included if possible.

For the subject index, the same alphabetization should occur before consolidation. One of the tricks of a subject index is to get the right balance between major and minor headings. This comes through knowledge of the subject and the experience of indexing itself.

Ancient sources have their own challenges in consolidating with regard to the declining pyramid of references. Different publishers have different practices in this regard as well, but a general rule is to have larger units before smaller units. So, returning to our example of Aeschylus's *The Agamemnon*, a set of entries after ordering and consolidation might read as follows:

Aeschylus, *Ag.*

135–282	17
135–142	12
135–137	19
141–143	136

The unit 135–282 is larger than 135–142 and 135–137, so for a publisher who uses a hierarchy of larger to smaller units, the entry would read as above.

There are a couple of tricks for alphabetizing that you should be aware of. Alphabetization can follow letter-by-letter or word-by-word alphabetization. The difference is whether you compare letter by letter as if there were no space between words, or whether you take the first word (excluding "the" or "a") and then at the break between words alphabetize these words separately. There are also some particular alphabetization issues regarding names. Some publishers put names with "Mac" and "Mc" together as if they were all "Mac," while others keep them separate. Some publishers treat the German umlaut as if it were the vowels u and e (e.g., $ü = u + e$), while others simply alphabetize according to the vowel alone. Publishers also have different criteria for handling such names as De Bruin, van Dijk, and the like, that is, whether they are found under D or B, or V or D.

Once all of these steps have been taken, I suggest that you print out each of the index lists and then edit them. I am always amazed to find how many inconsistencies I have missed while viewing the indexes on-screen. There may be cases where I have not consolidated all of the references to a given name, or where I have not handled the page extents of references correctly, and the like. All of these items need to be checked. There is more to indexing than this, but what publishers want is the index list or lists that you have prepared for the given book. They assume responsibility for taking the list, which usually can be submitted electronically, and setting it up according to their house style. Authors usually do not get a chance to proofread their indexes once they are sent to the publisher, so getting them right the first time is important.

A potential difficulty at this stage of publication can occur if there have been significant changes at proof stage that require changes in pagination. It only takes a couple of little changes for a reference to a modern author in a footnote to roll over to the next page, with a cascading effect on the manuscript and the indexes. If you think that this might be a potential problem, I think that it is wise to make sure the project manager (or production editor) of your volume knows, so that the editor can check the indexes to be sure they are accurate. Often typesetters can manipulate the setup of the page so that there is less rollover than you might expect. In any case, the time to check these matters of detail is before publication, not after.

Some Other Matters

Depending upon the nature of the individual publication, there may be other important matters to attend to as well. For most of these, the burden rests on the author to resolve the issues involved. I list three items here, but there may well be others.

Illustrations

Some works require illustrations. Besides the issue of gaining permission to use someone else's illustrations, there is the challenge of providing the illustrations in a form that can be adequately reproduced.

Charts and Graphs

Even if you create the charts and graphs on your own, you as the author need to ensure that they are in a form that can be reproduced clearly and well.

Copyrighted Material and Permissions

It is usually the author's responsibility to arrange for permission to reproduce copyrighted material. If there are fees involved, you can bet that the publisher will want you to pay them. Again, I am not a lawyer, so I cannot give legal advice, but my experience is that there is ambiguity between the protections of copyright and what constitutes fair use of copyrighted material. This has special pertinence for use of shorter works such as songs and poems, when citing only a line or two can be a major portion of the work. I recommend that you be sure that the publisher knows from the outset that such materials are being included, and get their recommendations and advice on how to handle such use. Sometimes all that is required is to write a simple and straightforward letter to the copyright holder, letting them know that you wish to use such material in a scholarly publication with limited circulation, and request permission for reproduction. Unfortunately, sometimes such copyright owners wish to be paid fees, in which case I would assess the fee, see if the publisher is willing to pay it, and see if there is a way to either negotiate a better deal or use some other work not covered by copyright.

Any author who has followed what has been said in this book to this point should be ready for success in developing a research and publishing profile. In light of this, it is entirely appropriate to prepare for the next step after acceptance. Publication does not begin and end with acceptance by a publisher of an article or book. There are important next steps to be handled as well. One of the major ones is proofreading. Proofreading can be a laborious and slow process, but it is one that is necessary to ensure that the work that goes out under our names is the best representation of our work that we can make it. Even though the publisher's name is on the book as well, our names are prominently displayed on them as authors, and our readers look to us for getting the details right. The same is true of indexes. The indexes are a further tool for aiding readers in gaining access to our work, and their accuracy and completeness help to ensure that readers find our work useful and worthwhile.

REPRESENTATIVE TIMES FOR VARIOUS STAGES IN PUBLISHING[4]

Journal Articles

Time from submission to decision	Three months to one year
Time from submission to publication	One to three years

Monographs and Books

Time from submission to decision	Three months to one year[5]
Time from acceptance to author's proofs	Six months to one year
Time from submission to publication	One to two years

Proofreading Rate

Number of pages proofread per hour   12–17
Range of time allowed for proofreading   Three days to one month

Index Preparation
(based on 100,000-word/250-page book)

Subject index   20 hours average (estimate)
Modern authors index   10 hours average (estimate)
Ancient sources index   15 hours average (estimate)

8

Will I Run Out of Publishable Ideas?

The short answer to this question is, "Almost assuredly no." When I was just finishing graduate school and beginning to publish, I wondered whether I would run out of ideas for further publishing. I had done a couple of articles, and had a couple more in preparation, and I was finishing my doctoral dissertation and had a publisher for that work. I couldn't help but wonder, however, whether, when all of this was done, I would be able to think of anything further to write on. What if I couldn't? What would I do then? I continued to work on the projects that I was involved in, and one idea led to another, and soon I got a couple of invitations to write on something, and then I set some further goals for myself. Soon other invitations started to come in, and my curiosity got the best of me and I started to explore areas that branched out from my initial interests—until one day I realized what I very much know now. I have so many good ideas for publishing projects that there is no way that I will ever finish all of them unless I live a lot longer than I expect to. The problem is not whether I will run out of ideas, but whether I will run out of time to do all that I currently have planned, to say nothing of completing other projects that keep coming my way. The more work that I do, the more ideas come along. One time not too long ago, I surveyed one of my bookcases to peruse some books, and thought that I would write down ideas for a couple of potential articles that were related to this group of books. I filled an entire sheet of paper with viable ideas after only looking at one shelf of books, and turned away disheartened, because I realized I had set my sights far too low—there were far more ideas than I could ever get to researching and writing.

You may be thinking that it is easy for me to be saying this now, but there was a time in the past—as I have admitted above—when I was not sure that I would be able to keep the ideas flowing and the pace of publication going. I have several recommendations to make to help generate new publishing ideas. I am assuming that your dissertation has been written with the idea of publication in mind and has become the first major book that you have published. Finding other sources of new ideas can involve many different means, including the following: (1) the use of graduate research papers, (2) delivery of conference papers, (3) spin-offs from other projects, (4) solicitations, (5) edited volumes, and (6) the exploration of new areas.

Graduate Research Papers

As graduate students, most scholars have had to write a lot of academic papers. In fact, they probably have written at least one major paper for each of their graduate seminars. In the course of their graduate career, this probably means they have taken a minimum of somewhere around six to twenty different courses, depending on the number and type of degrees earned. If you were a fortunate graduate student, you studied with professors who challenged you to undertake new and frontline research in your courses and pushed you to write papers suitable for publication. I am still surprised at how many graduate-level faculty do not encourage their students to start looking to publish the papers they produce in their courses. I was fortunate that I had a couple of first-rate professors who did encourage me in this way; however, some of my colleagues were not so encouraged, and others simply did not take advantage of the opportunities as they came along.

My first published article, as I have mentioned above, was a form of a revised paper from a course that I took. The professor had very strict guidelines for the presentation of the paper to the class, but the demands of the course meant that we were definitely doing work on the forefront of the discipline. This time was the advent of the use of computer databases for our field of study, and so each student was required to do a project that utilized such a database. Quite clearly, with a little thought and ingenuity, each student would have a piece of work that brought discussion of the topic to a new level through the use of computer technology. Of course, we were not thinking of this at the time, but we were simply trying to find a topic and get a paper done. At the end of the course, the professor noted that he believed that three of the papers that had been delivered by students in the course could, with proper revision, be published. Mine was one of the three. To my knowledge, to this day, I was the only one of the three students who talked with him further about getting their paper published, and it was. This was a missed opportunity by all of the other students in the class, and especially by the two others who had received such favorable encouragement. I was able to publish a total of five papers that came out of work done during my graduate study, not counting two that were first delivered at conferences during my time as a student that were later published.

This situation did not always work out so well, however. I remember preparing a paper for one course during my studies, where I consciously wished to head toward publication, and discussed this prospect with my professor. At the end of the day, what I came up with was not publishable in either his or my eyes, so I never did anything further with this paper. What was the difference between the two papers, one that was and one that was not good enough for publication?

There are several factors that I think make the diffcrence. One is the orientation to the subject. In each of the instances that resulted in publication, I had an orientation to the subject that was distinctly different in some definable, measurable, and perceivable way from the standard viewpoint on the topic. I believe that this clear difference gives the article a better chance for publication, because a reviewer can see that the manuscript makes a contribution to knowledge. Another factor is the useful guidance of a professor along the way. By now, if you are already out of graduate school and on the way to developing your career, it is too late to wish your professors had given more guidance. If you are reading this book while you are a graduate student, now is the time to start cultivating relationships with professors who can and will encourage you in publication. This does not necessarily mean that they are the heaviest hitters on the faculty (my experience is that some of these are the stingiest with their help and encouragement), but it should be someone who has an interest in publishing, who has done enough of it to know how it is done, and who is interested in helping you develop your research profile. For those of you who are already out of graduate school, you should try to think back to see if there was a professor who encouraged you in various ways, and whose influence may well have been transferred into the written work that you did, such that that work may well have the germ of a publishable piece in it. A third factor is simply the nature of the discipline itself and whether your work addresses the kinds of issues being discussed. You will need to take a hardheaded approach to evaluating your work to see if it is suitable for spending time getting it into shape for possible publication.

Conference Papers

Conference papers constitute one of the best sources of papers for possible publication. As I mention above, I always try to go to a conference with my paper complete, including footnotes, and ready for publication. At the conference itself, I often catch a few typographical errors, may be informed of a key reference that I need to check, or may be compelled by discussion and argument to reexamine a position. But these are relatively small fine-tunings compared to the actual preparation of a paper. So far as I can, when I take a paper to a conference I take a paper that I believe is suitable to turn over to a publisher—just in case an editor or publisher approaches me after the session and asks for it.[1] By contrast, I know a colleague who loves the thrill of spontaneous paper delivery. In other words, he rarely prepares thoroughly in advance, but often stays up the night before to prepare a PowerPoint presentation. He delivers a very engaging paper, but finds it exceptionally difficult to get some of them published, because they do not actually exist except as an oral performance. Once the performance is over, the so-called "paper" is also over, so he moves on to other things, and these papers will probably never see print publication.

Giving papers at conferences can be a great source for publication ideas and, more than that, a great vehicle for producing the papers themselves. I have given over a dozen conference papers in each of several years. I was very busy writing on average one publishable paper a month, but the experience was also very rewarding and helped to advance my research profile. My policy, at least for a while in the early days of my career, was to initiate and accept every scholarly paper-giving opportunity that I could. I could not sustain this, but it started my career on the right track.

There are a couple of different types of conferences at which you may give a paper. The first type of conference is one for which a general invitation is given for papers. Most professional societies or organizations of scholars in a particular field have such conferences. I like the idea of a conference that affords the opportunity for wide-open participation, because it gives me a chance to try out all sorts of different ideas in an environment where they will usually be given immediate constructive response and feedback by my peers. This is like hiring a professional coach but without the fee. Your peers who are interested in your topic—that is the reason that they are usually present at the sessions—show up and hear your paper and are willing to ask questions, give constructive comments, and even talk with you later about what you have to say, all in the interest of your producing a better paper. Such conversations often also lead to suggestions regarding publication. One of those interested in the paper may be on the editorial board of a journal or monograph series, or even be the editor of one of these, and may express serious interest in publishing your paper as an article in the journal, or even having you develop it into a book-length treatment.

For a conference such as this, you will need to generate the idea that you wish to research and write about, but it provides a great opportunity to do this work. I would suggest that in such contexts you feel free to explore new areas that you have been interested in but have not yet had the opportunity to pursue. You may find that it opens up a whole new area of exploration, leading to several articles or even a book. Or you may find that the area is one that you are not interested in after all, or that you come to believe you cannot or are not willing to make a contribution to. In that case, all that you have done is spent some time on a single paper—but I would still make every effort to get the paper published. I have made it a habit over the last several years to propose a paper on a different angle or perspective on one topic of interest at a general conference each year. Each time, my proposal has been accepted, and I have delivered the paper. I have had at least one of these unpublished papers already favorably cited in another publication as providing a solution to an interpretive problem, and now I have enough papers—all of these previously unpublished conference papers—to assemble a book on the topic.

Another type of conference is one at which there is a general or broad topic selected for the conference. These conferences also provide a useful opportunity for generation of ideas and potential publications. Such conferences are often organized by professional societies and groups of scholars for their membership. The organizing topic can provide stimulation to think along particular lines for those wishing to present papers. This often can be the impetus that is needed for preparing a paper in a new

...ea of exploration. I mentioned just above that I had prepared a number of papers on various angles of a chosen topic. Some of these papers were delivered at conferences that had designated topics. I used these topics to provide the angle that I would explore for my particular subject. I figured that the conference title would provide the new direction for my approach to my topic, and that gearing the paper to the conference area certainly would not hurt in getting my paper accepted for delivery at the conference. I was never disappointed, as all of my proposals that were geared to the topic of the conference were accepted. I don't necessarily suggest, however, that you try what I tried early on in my career. Early on, there was a themed conference, and I was a young scholar with no name or reputation, so I decided that one way to enhance my chances of getting a paper proposal accepted was to put the topic of the conference into my paper title. I did so and had the paper proposal accepted. After I had delivered the paper, the first questioner asked, "What does your paper have to do with the subject of the conference?" I had to admit that it really didn't have any, but that I had used it as a way of getting the paper proposal accepted. He was not pleased with my paper or my response. The paper itself, incidentally, was accepted by a refereed international journal almost by return mail—I suspect that the journal editor himself accepted it—and it was published in due course. It stimulated quite a bit of response in various quarters. At one conference a number of years later, I was approached by a well-known senior scholar who asked me what I had done to get my paper accepted and published in this particular journal—as if this were some rare occurrence that was an enigma to him. I said that I really had no idea, except that I had sent the paper to them. There was a good lesson in that, I thought—if you don't submit papers, it is unlikely you will get them accepted and published.

A third type of conference is one that is organized solely around smaller subgroups, and it is a requirement that you submit a paper to a particular subgroup. I personally do not like this type of conference, because I believe that it has a prescriptive and stultifying effect on scholarship. It is too easy to break down the discipline into personal "old boys" groups that control the various areas of the discipline, so that they only let in a certain crowd to play on their field. The other effect of such organization is to limit the possibilities of scholars undertaking research in areas with which they are not identified. If the organizers of the various subgroups are looking for certain established people to give papers in their field, in order to "guarantee" the quality (or audience?) of a particular session, they may not be as inclined to accept a proposal by someone who is not known for work in that area. One of the odd things about recent scholarship in some fields is that there is a small number of guru figures whose names are commonly known but who may not be that expert any more (if they were to begin with), since they have sold out to writing trade books or writing for very popular audiences or even writing on anything and everything that comes along, whether they have a legitimate or worthwhile opinion or not. The vast majority of scholars are not that well known apart from their area of expertise, and so it is difficult for them to get name recognition apart from within their narrow area.[2] Despite all of this, these conferences are still penetrable but require a little more diligence. I recommend that you make early contact with the various subarea organizers or coordinators and find out what they are looking for or need for their particular sessions. The area might also require that you do more research in advance of making your proposal. This is not necessarily a bad thing, as it may enable you to head off investing a lot of time and energy in an area that ends up not being of interest to you. Nevertheless, the nature of such subgroups helps to define subject areas for papers, and so I would encourage you to submit proposals to them as a means of developing paper topics. You as a potential contributor are forced to fit your paper proposal into one of the areas of the conference—short of proposing a whole new area, which you may well do sometime along the way—and thereby introduce yourself to a new and potentially productive area of scholarly research.

A fourth type of conference is the conference geared around a particularly narrow and defined topic or even theme. These kinds of conferences are different from the ones above in that, rather than having a number of different subareas within the larger scholarly field, they are more like having a conference on just one of the areas. If such a conference has an open call for papers, it is up to you to show to the organizers that you can make a contribution to the discussion. It may be that such a conference is tangentially related to your previous area or areas of research, or provides a new perspective on the subject. I would use such an angle or angles as a way to formulate your proposal for the conference. It may be that you have no previous acquaintance with the topic, except that you now are very interested in the subject and wish to explore it in more detail. This will probably require more preparatory work on your part, because you need to get up to speed on the state of research, but such an effort may well have publishable rewards. It is often those who are new to an area who provide some of the best and most important insights, because they are not fully acculturated to the discipline and do not know that one is not supposed to ask particular questions or to explore particular areas that are thought to be fully and finally settled. This new perspective alone may be useful both for stimulating your interest in the topic and for creating interest in your participation in the conference, and hence may result in presentation of a paper.

Earlier in my career, I responded to a call for papers for a conference in a particular area that I had no particular interest in or knowledge of. I am not sure why I did it, except that it seemed like they were going to meet in an exciting place. I also had the advantage that I knew something about publishing, which the organizers did not want to be bothered with, and so I suggested that I could help get the conference proceedings published. They accepted both my offer regarding involvement in publication and my paper proposal. It turns out that my paper ended up being a critical estimation of the field that discouraged the kind of work that the majority of participants in the conference were involved in. Perhaps it was because I was presenting a contrarian view, or perhaps it was because I saw to it that five volumes were eventually published from these conferences, but I was invited back and even became one of the organizers of the conferences. A number of years after I quit being involved with this field and its conferences, I still get invitations to write on this subject area—because my name is associated with it, even though I am not particularly supportive of the governing orientation.

The final conference type I will mention is the invited paper or papers. It may be that you are the only one invited, or you may be invited along with a number of others, but I usually have only one answer to give when such invitations come my way: "yes." Conferences such as this sometimes leave the topic open to the speaker, or, more times than not, they will prescribe an area that they wish for you to explore. Often such conferences include publication of the conference papers. As long as I think that I can make a reasonably good attempt at the topic assigned to me, I accept such invitations. Many of them also come with some or all of my expenses paid, so I really have very little to lose, and as a result I have visited some very nice places and met some very nice people—and had some very nice publications. This kind of conference is one of the two most common types of conferences that I have organized (the other being the conference with a specific theme but open paper submissions within that theme). These are good conferences to organize, because they make a focused and concentrated contribution to the topic. All of the contributors have their general areas assigned, and the end product generally covers the range of major areas within the field of exploration. Such conferences often make good edited collections of papers for publishers. They overcome some of the hesitations that publishers have with collections of essays such as *Festschriften*, which have no clear focus to them because they address a single academic area. Some of these volumes not only make a scholarly contribution but have the potential for use as textbooks as well. Usually a potential contributor will be asked to participate on the basis of established expertise in the area, but sometimes that person will be asked on the basis of general subject expertise or for some other reason. If it is a field that you are already expert in, such a conference gives an occasion to get another publication without too much new effort, perhaps refining or focusing some of your work in new ways. If it is an area that you are not already expert in, such a conference gives an occasion to explore a new area; benefit from interaction with others, some of whom will have expertise in the subject; and consequently get a publication as well.

The most unusual experience I have had with a conference of this type was when I was invited to respond to a particular featured speaker. The conference itself had generated an open invitation to this speaker, but then I had been asked to be one of two respondents to the speaker's lectures. The major difficulty was that I was to respond to the speaker two months before he actually gave his set of lectures for the conference. This unusual set of circumstances gave me the opportunity to prepare some comments in direct response to the speaker, but also to explore some of the other areas of the topic, knowing in advance that he was not going to speak about them (I had been sent a copy of his papers in advance). I think that overall it came off very well, with inclusion in a publication that has been cited in a number of different venues and used as a course text.

Participation in conferences of various types can be one of the most productive ways of generating new ideas for publications. The opportunity to deliver a paper for comment and critique in advance of submission for possible publication virtually guarantees that this is a risk-free area of potential productivity.

Spin-Offs from Other Projects

One of the temptations of young scholars is to believe that somewhere in their first articles, and even monographs, they must say everything that there is to say about a subject. As an editor of several monograph series, including ones that publish doctoral dissertations, I think that I know where this tendency comes from. The tendency comes from the kind of atmosphere that is all too often created in doctoral study, where the student dare not say anything without saying everything—including citing every scholar who even dared to have a private thought about the subject. That pattern may have been sufficient for doctoral study—although I have my doubts, as I have noted in chapter 1—but it is not a good way to approach the creation of a publishing profile.

There are several major tenets for creating a good publishing profile, and one of them is that you should never hope to say everything about a subject in one article, chapter, or volume. First of all, it is an idealistic and probably unachievable and unattainable goal anyway, and so the result is bound to be frustrating—and may well end up with you never publishing at all because of the fear that you do not say the last word. The second factor is that it leaves nothing more to be said on other occasions. Another tenet of creating a good publishing profile is that most subject areas are still in constant development and subject to scrutiny, and any idea of a final stasis is unreasonable, unlikely, and, in fact, not to be welcomed. Such a state would mean that perfect and ultimate knowledge has been gained. This not only defies logic and experience, but it has a disheartening and dampening effect on the scholarly endeavor. Instead, you as a writing scholar should welcome the fact that there is always going to be more to say about any discipline. In fact, you should be open to the situation in which you may well change your mind in print, from a position held earlier in your career to a different opinion later. Though such changes could become capricious, if you have genuinely rethought the issue and changed your mind, I would not hesitate to publish that result.

The spin-offs from any previous work should be a constant source of new ideas for publications. Sometimes these spin-offs are merely a means of filling out footnotes from previous publications. By that, I mean that sometimes an idea or concept is suggested in a publication that cannot be fully developed at the time. Sometimes reference will be made to such a concept in a footnote. Subsequent publications are an ideal venue for filling out these footnotes and developing these ideas more fully. At other times, these spin-offs can be major points in the development of a series of ideas regarding a subject. For example, you might consider a single, massive article in which the full state of play of a subject is discussed. Or, instead, you might even propose a single book on the subject. Perhaps it might be better, if possible, to divide the field up into its several parts and write an article, or even an entire book, on each one of these. I know of instances where this has been attempted. One outstanding and innovative scholar developed a model for communications theory and wrote the first of three proposed volumes on each of the three major parts of his theory. Unfortunately, the Nazi invasion of his country leading up to World War II meant that he was never able to complete his tripartite project, but it was an excellent idea nevertheless. And at still other times, spin-offs can spin pretty far away from the center of the subject, depending upon the circumstances and opportunities. Spin-offs can come about as the result of simply blue-sky thinking about a particular discipline. Once you have established your knowledge in a given field, it is possible to think creatively about some of the implications and possible directions of that field. If there are interesting avenues and connections that have not been explored before, or that have been explored only in unsatisfactory ways, then these are areas that can lead to whole new fields of scholarly publication.

Solicitations

There are any number of reasons that a scholar may be asked by others to write on a given topic. Some of these reasons make logical and understandable sense—a scholar is the best-known figure in that field, or has published the most important recent article or book in the area, or has given a stimulating paper at a recent conference on the very topic, or the like. There are also a number of other, less understandable and even illogical, reasons that some scholars are asked—this scholar was confused with someone else with a name something like it, someone confused this scholar with someone else at the same institution or a college with a name something like it, someone was going through a directory of scholars in the field and landed on this one, they needed to address the politically correct balance of their project and so chose someone they thought fit that profile, they thought they remembered that this scholar had at one time done a paper or book or something on this or a related topic, they (or a friend) met this scholar once and were favorably impressed by him or her, this scholar asked to be included in any projects that were being put together, or this scholar is a friend.

The truth of the matter is that I have been either the recipient of invitations or the selector of participants in publishing projects for virtually all of the reasons, logical and illogical, mentioned above. If you are in the scholarship business very long, you may well be also. We may not like these reasons, and in fact we may even find some of them disgusting, but the truth is that when it comes to needing someone to write an article or a chapter for a conference or a book, the primary motivation is coming up with the name of someone who will do it—and often who will do it fast.

There are a number of such writing projects that have highly intensive contributor needs. I mentioned above that I ended up being assigned around forty entries to write for a major dictionary project simply on the basis of asking the editor for the opportunity and writing a couple of good articles quickly. This led to my writing the rest of them. I have also myself been an editor of several major reference works. All of these required multiple contributors, and, as these projects got closer to the deadline for submission, there were always those who were not able to come up with the article that they had promised several years earlier. For one such project, I had to write an article that had been promised for five years on the last night before submission, simply because this person did not come through as promised and I could not find someone who would do it on such short notice (twenty-four hours is indeed short notice). Therefore, I believe that you as an aspiring publishing scholar should make sure that as many people as possible are informed that you are available and ready to write, even without much advance warning.

I am constantly amazed at how many young scholars will beg off on publishing opportunities because they say they are too busy. Too busy with what? I interpret this to mean that they are unwilling to give up a few hours of edifying television or jogging or paintball in order to secure a publication—often one that even pays a little money. When I was editing my most recent reference work, I drew on a number of graduate students for contributions, because they were willing and able to write the articles needed on short notice. The quality of their work was often as good as that by more senior scholars (sometimes even better!) and virtually always good enough for such a reference tool—and certainly better than no article at all, which was all some of my senior colleagues managed.

Once you become known as a scholar who can produce the goods on demand, other invitations will come. Some of these may well be in the same area as the articles written for these reference works. On the basis of the articles that I wrote for a dictionary some years ago, I still get occasional invitations to write articles on related subjects. These invitations will often extend way beyond simple dictionary or encyclopedia or other reference work articles, because there are all kinds of projects that often need contributors. These might include special issues of journals, geared around a particular theme or topic with which you may have some expertise or interest. Many publishers like to produce books that contain substantive articles that describe the state of play of a field. If you are known as one of the leaders in the field, you may be asked to write one of these articles. If you let it be known to others that you are interested, this probably will increase your chances—especially if you deliver the article on time and as asked. Some other publishers do a lot of edited collections of essays geared around particular topics. Sometimes these are even established in series that give potential contributors an idea of what topics are forthcoming. This provides an opportunity to be invited to contribute to such an ongoing publication.

As I mentioned above with requests to contribute to conferences, my standard answer for contributing to any publishing project is "yes." I think later about what I might say in the article. Such an opportunity often gives me the chance to do not only this particular piece but others that may come to mind or come about as a result.

Edited Volumes

I have mentioned above edited volumes of essays that might generate solicitations for contributions and to which you as an aspiring publishing scholar may be able to contribute. Another way of generating ideas for publications is through the process of editing volumes of essays by others. Many publishers like to publish such collections—although not all publishers, especially during tough economic times. Some publishers do not like edited collections, because they believe that these collections lack a unified perspective on a particular topic, and they do not sell as well as monographs. Besides the fact that these decisions are being made simply on the basis of money (the single most important factor that drives the publishing industry), there are ways to address this situation. One means is to be sure that the topic of the volume is focused and specific so that commissioning editors and potential buyers will recognize the topic and its importance without question. A second approach is to see if you can place such an edited volume within a series produced by the publisher, or even establish this volume as the basis of a series itself. Books in series for most academic publishers sell far better than individual volumes. The logic to this is simple. If a publisher sells a series, the salesperson only has to sell it once, and then the series itself sells every other book in it, thus cutting back on sales and advertising costs, and perhaps even the cost of the book itself (perhaps this last hope is a little optimistic). Each and every particular individual or freestanding book requires a concerted sales effort. There is not even the same kind of residual or backlist sales potential for individual volumes as there is for a series that keeps on going, and for which there may continue to be backlog demand as new subscribers join the series. A third means to generate interest in such a collection is to ensure that there are some big-name people contributing to the edited volume. As one publisher I used to work with astutely said, "I publish most of the biggest names in the field," by having their papers in collections of essays. It may be impossible to get one of these well-known scholars to write a monograph for a particular publisher, but it may well be possible for you to get the author to write an article or chapter for your collection of essays. This gets the name recognition attached to the volume, and the scholar doesn't have to write an entire book to make a contribution.

So far, what I have been saying is focused more on justifying the publication of edited volumes, whereas this section is really meant to be geared toward generating further ideas for publication by an aspiring scholar. The key here is for you to be the one who is generating the ideas for the edited volumes and then developing the projects and seeing them through to publication. As the scholar wanting to develop publishing ideas, you are forced to think of new ideas for volumes that will meet a particular need in the market, or address a particular issue that is of importance in the field. This effort has the effect of stimulating perhaps a whole slew of new ideas for the given academic discipline, addressed by various contributors to the volume. As the editor of the volume, and as the scholar who wants to develop a research profile, you definitely should be one of the contributors to such a volume. I have edited over fifty-five volumes, and I think that I have been a contributor to all but one where the essays were new essays and not simply reprinted essays from previous publications. That is the prerogative of the editor of the volume—to be one of the contributors. More than that, the editor usually gets the choice of topics to write on and helps to control the nature and type of the other essays that are included. A final benefit of such a project is that it may well lead to the development of further ideas for publication, whether this is a freestanding journal article, another collection of essays, or even a monograph on the topic.

New Areas of Exploration

One of the questions that all scholars must ask themselves is how specialized they are going to be and how long they are going to continue to be that specialized. There are scholars who are content to have a single major area of intellectual and academic exploration and to continue in that area for their entire career. They are often known as the go-to person for this area, and there is nothing major in the field that goes on without their knowledge and possibly even participation. They come to be identified with the field, and there is even a time sometime along the way when they become one of the central figures in this area, probably editing journals and monograph series and sitting on numerous editorial boards. They are entirely satisfied with this, and they like the kind of recognition that it brings, as well as the continued opportunities for publication that go along with such an established position.

Here is not the place to debate the merits or demerits of pursuing such a career path, as much of it may be based on education, opportunity, situation, and temperament, as on anything else. Instead, the situation I want to address is that of the aspiring scholar faced with such a possible scenario but wondering whether there will be enough new developments to continue to be stimulated by and interested in a single field to the exclusion of others. On the basis of what I have been saying, it is entirely possible simply to pursue a single area and to do well as a publishing and contributing scholar. Numerous areas of scholarship are full of such scholarly profiles.

If you are set on developing and exploring radically new ideas that continue to flow through to publication, then you probably need to determine how specialized you wish to be and how long you wish to remain so. I mentioned above that I have been criticized for not having a single focus to my scholarship—even though I have published more than some established experts in a number of different areas. Apart from the issue of how you are perceived and how you perceive yourself with regard to the profession, I would recommend that being curious about numerous areas is certainly the best way to continue to generate new ideas for publication. This means that you can only stay focused on a single, specific discipline for so long before you need to turn your attention to other areas. There is something creative in simply turning your attention to another area, bringing a fresh set of eyes to focus on a discipline, and drawing upon your outsider perspective and background, that almost inevitably is bound to bring new insights to bear on a given field. These new insights then need to be developed into publications.

The short answer to the question of whether young scholars interested in developing a research profile will run out of ideas is "no." It is not likely. However, there are a number of easy and straightforward steps that you can take to ensure that this is not even a reasonable question. Most of these suggestions boil down to the simple strategy of taking advantage of every opportunity that is presented—whether that is in terms of using work previously done, making proposals for various types of conferences, developing spin-off ideas, taking advantage of invitations, editing books, or simply undertaking to learn a new area of academic expertise. All of them begin with you looking for and responding to opportunities, but can end up with you being given and taking advantage of more opportunities than you can ever imagine.

9

LIVING A PUBLISHING LIFESTYLE

A publishing lifestyle is not simply a lifestyle developed early in your academic career and then abandoned once you have secured tenure. A publishing lifestyle involves constantly seeking to make a serious contribution to your field of academic endeavor, from first appointment to emeritus status and beyond. This means that it is not an "added extra" to life, or something that you have to think twice about before undertaking, or behavior to be turned on or off at will. A publishing lifestyle is an intentional lifestyle that believes that—all of the vagaries and jokes regarding the scholarly world, publishing included, aside—the individual scholar who is dedicated to an academic field can and will be making a regular and steady contribution to the development of learning and understanding. This contribution is not judged in terms of publicity, pseudocelebrity appearances on the television or radio, citations in the popular press, or popular-level publications. It is determined by the serious research and writing that genuinely advances knowledge. Those who sell out for popular appeal soon become the tired hacks that they seek to emulate, but serious scholarship is beneficial not only for its own time but for other times as well. It endures long after the lights have faded, the print has blurred, and the channel has been changed. Such serious scholarship endures longer than the very scholars themselves and becomes the foundation for a subsequent generation of scholars who themselves are pushing the frontiers of knowledge even further forward. This is not an idealized picture of scholarship, because we all know that along the way there are various abortive attempts, questionable motives, and some wrong dealing. What I am speaking of is the scholarship that stands the test of time, even if it is not recognized in its own time, and becomes the intellectual foundations of continuing intellectual endeavor.

I wish here to identify four principles of a publishing lifestyle that I believe will help to ensure its continued success for the one who practices it. These four include (1) setting goals, (2) the rule of five and one, (3) the "never say no" principle, and (4) avoiding the paralysis of overanalysis.

Setting Goals

When I had my first academic position, I wanted to be sure that I did not fall into the trap that so many young professors do, of spending so much time on course preparation that I let my research go cold. I had invested a good number of years in developing my primary subject expertise, and I wanted to be sure that I was able to have the most enduring kind of impact on my primary field as I could while my research was still fresh and I was still able to say a number of things that had not been said in the field before. I realized that I would have to exercise discipline, especially in these early days of my career, if I was to be able to fulfill the general goals that I had for my contribution to my field. As a result, I set a number of specific goals for myself. There were two goals that focused on my publications. One was to start a pattern of getting books published on a regular basis, and the other was to start getting articles published in major and significant refereed journals. In these early stages, I figured that if I paid attention to these two dimensions, other areas would work themselves out, such as giving conference papers and the like. As it turned out, they did.

In the early stages of my publishing career, I went about publishing my dissertation as quickly and straightforwardly as possible. It was more difficult to set goals for myself regarding publication in journals. What I finally stumbled upon was to establish a pattern that fit my particular area of primary research interest but that might not fit with other fields. However, it gives a good idea of the kinds of goals that you can set and the time frame in which to accomplish them. My primary field of research activity and interest is a field that draws together scholars from all over the world, but in particular from North America and Europe. So I decided that I would select what I considered to be the premier journals in my field in the Western world. I selected one journal published in the USA by the premier North American professional organization in my field; the premier journal in the UK, also published by the premier European and now international professional organization in my field (the organization requires that members be nominated for membership but does not require membership to publish in their journal—my membership came a number of years later); the premier journal in the Netherlands; the one in Germany; and the one in Italy. I could have added other major journals to the list, but, for those who know the field, these five would probably be on most everyone's list of top-level journals. I also set myself a specific goal of getting my work published in each of these journals in the course of my career. However, once I set out on this endeavor and met with initial success, I revised this goal to getting published in these journals as soon as possible, and no longer than in the next five years or so. In order to do this, I had to identify the specific requirements of the journals, formulate an idea of the right paper to write for each journal, submit the papers for publication, and then see them through to their appearance.

I was able to do all of this so that within four years I had publications in all five of the journals, from conception of the ideas to the articles appearing in print. The article in the journal in the USA was one that started as a conference paper I delivered a couple of times and the one that I had to revise thoroughly with the help of my friend the poet and novelist. It was the one that took the longest to get published. The one published in the journal in the UK was a revised form of a paper delivered at one of my first professional conferences in my field upon completion of my Ph.D. After having that paper scrutinized by an invited respondent at that conference, I was confident that it would meet the standards of an anonymous reviewer, and it did. It was accepted fairly quickly. The paper for the journal in the Netherlands was one that I wrote as a result of some of the teaching that I was doing in my early years. As I developed a particular course, I became aware of a particular issue and wrote up a paper that addressed the topic. This paper too was accepted fairly readily. The paper that was accepted for publication in the German journal originally was not designed for publication in that journal but was an article that was rejected by another well-known journal. This rejection solved the problem of what I would submit to the German journal, and it was readily accepted. This paper had also grown out of preparation for a course that I was teaching. The fifth paper appeared in the Italian journal. This paper was written for the same professional conference at which I delivered one of my first papers mentioned above, but was delivered two years later. Even though I had to reduce the paper by a couple of pages, the publisher was very fast, and the article appeared the next year.

indeed fortunate to be in a situation where both my teaching
opportunities to deliver conference papers could lead to publica-
elieve that the major factor in my getting these papers published,
however, was the fact that I had set a clear and definable goal and set out
to accomplish it. I had identified what it was I was trying to accomplish,
knew what it would take to accomplish such a goal, and then took the
necessary steps to achieve it. I don't know that anyone I was working
with knew that this was my goal. It was not the kind of goal that people
saw me scurrying about each day to accomplish. However, as I thought
through what I was teaching and which conference papers I would try to
give, I was keeping an eye on getting papers published in these journals.
As it turned out, during this time I also was able to get articles published
in a number of other refereed journals—after all, I was trying to develop
a publishing lifestyle, and so the success of my specific goal had the
wider effect of carrying over into a variety of other activities and accom-
plishments that helped me to fulfill this ambition. A number of years ago,
I set a new goal for myself that I am still working toward. My goal now
is that, before I retire, I want to have published something of significance
on the primary texts in my field. So far I have published an article, chapter, or book (in which there is a specific chapter on one of these texts) on
three-quarters of them. I am well on the way to reaching my goal, and I
am developing opportunities to publish on the final number of texts.

Rule of Five and One

One of the major questions that arises in a variety of venues is how you
as a scholar determine whether you are making a contribution to your
field. This is a very difficult and highly subjective question to answer,
as there are so many variables involved. There are some who believe
that popular appeal is the measure of success. I seriously doubt that this
is true, because very little of the popular so-called scholarship is really
innovative or creative scholarship. It is instead usually a summary of
received opinions, often toned down for more general consumption, and
it has little lasting value. There are others who believe that name recognition is the standard for determining success as a scholar. I am even more
skeptical of this, because reputation can be gained for all sorts of different things and at different times and in different ways—a good bit of it
having little to nothing to do with actual scholarship. Others think that
academic rank or institution is the mark of success in scholarship. This

is perhaps the least accurate measure of scholarly contribution, especially in a system where there is tenure that can serve to protect scholars from serious accomplishment.

In the course of my career, as an active academic, as a member of various search committees, and then as an administrator responsible for hiring, one of the things that I have tried to do is determine a way to gauge whether a scholar is an active and continuing contributor to scholarly research. This is not an easy task, as we all recognize that significance comes in a variety of packages. I have been able, I think, to determine at least one measure of scholarly contribution. I do not claim that it is the only or even necessarily the best means, but it is one measure that I have found very helpful. I arrived at this estimation through two sets of observations. The first was in terms of one of the goals that I set for myself early on. Once I had the hang of getting my first book published, and then of getting a number of articles in print, I intuitively grasped what it meant to be developing a publishing lifestyle. I firmly believe that a publishing lifestyle means regular and periodic contributions to a field of study. The second observation was in terms of the lack of impetus that I witnessed in some other scholars around me. Some scholars claim that they are those who only write big books. For them, so they argue, this means that they should be left alone for a decade or two while they produce their great magnum opus. There are a few scholars who have produced such work, but not nearly as many as those who claim to be working on this giant monstrosity. There are other scholars who claim that the academic climate that we live in today dictates that they only publish articles and not books anymore. After all, so the claim goes, the scholarly world changes so fast that it makes the book obsolete, and we need to be putting out only our tentative and quickly adapting articles. For many of these scholars, it is indeed too difficult for them to keep up with the field, but that is not because of the field, I fear. These two observations pushed me to find a means of assessing a progressive and continuous contribution to scholarship, both for evaluation of myself and comparison with others.

I have concluded that it is important for scholars to be actively engaged in their discipline by periodically producing significant, major publications such as monographs, linked together by regular smaller publications in the field, such as articles and chapters. As a result, I set a goal for myself that I would attempt to publish at the pace of a monograph or authored book every five years, and an article or a chapter in a book every year. That seemed to me like a reasonable pace to mark significant accomplishment.[1] When it is stated in that way, it actually does not seem like very much, does it? Let me state it another way. If you as a scholar begin your career at thirty years old (and assuming it takes the first five years to get your first book out, as some recommend)[2] and retire at sixty-five, if you meet this requirement you will have published seven books and thirty-five articles.[3] Now, I realize that perhaps there are some fields where books are genuinely not published anymore, or are not the primary vehicles for capturing significant scholarship. In that case, you will need to find suitable equivalents, perhaps by doubling the number of articles or chapters. Also, in some disciplines where there is widely shared author-ship, there perhaps needs to be an equation so that more articles are required the further down the list of contributing authors you appear. In this calculation, I do not include edited books, except if there is a chapter of substance that I have written in it, which counts as an authored chap-ter, and I do not count dictionary or encyclopedia articles, book reviews, conference papers, or anything written strictly for the popular press.

Despite these limitations on the number of publications that count toward this total, this goal of a book every five years and an article or a chapter every year seemed to me to be reasonable, and so I set out to keep this pace. I actually published my seventh authored or coauthored book and my thirty-fifth journal article or chapter by the time I was about thirteen years into my post-Ph.D. career and about forty-three years old (by the time I had published my seventh authored book, I actually had over sixty articles and chapters). I have gone well beyond that by now. But I still hold to my original and, I think, reasonable goal and strive to produce a published book every five years and an article or chapter every year. My own experience indicates that this kind of publishing pace is a reasonable and reachable goal. In the time crunch that the academic world has become, I believe that it is more important than ever to set goals for our careers, whether these are in the areas of teaching or research. Fail-ure to set such goals usually means that any significant achievement will only be accidental. I would not want to think of this calculation as a rigid straitjacket that means that you cannot take a little more time to do the great book, or that it becomes the goal in itself of scholarship. However, I think that it is an accurate and reasonable way to determine whether a person is making a regular scholarly contribution to the field.

As a result, I have come to develop and use a variant of this formula in my scrutiny of candidates for jobs, and as a formula that can be used in tenure or similar reviews. The above formula basically means that an authored book is given a publishing value of five points and is worth five articles or chapters, which are each worth one point (I discuss some of the reasons for this in chapter 1). Therefore, a scholar who is producing at a reasonable pace should be averaging two publications a year (one-fifth of a book, or one point, and one article, or one point, each year). If we go back to the example of a scholar who begins at age thirty and retires at sixty-five with seven books and thirty-five articles or chapters, this means that the scholar has published material with a weight of seventy points (7 books × 5 = 35 + 35 articles or chapters). If that scholar has been active for thirty-five years, that means that the scholar averages two publications per year. I think that an average of two per year is a reasonable and attainable goal.

A scholar who wants to evaluate progress in their field can easily run the calculations. I suggest using the start date of when you finished the Ph.D. or secured your first permanent academic job and calculate from there, including the publications since that time weighted according to the simple formula I have provided. My average during the time that it took to reach publication of my first seven authored books and sixty or so articles was nearly eight per year, or over three times what I believe indicates a consistent publishing profile. Incidentally, if I had never published anything since then, my average would still be over four for my entire career to date. This indicates the importance of maintaining continuous publication, because even though my average would still be over twice the standard I have set, I would not have published for about nine years (however, I have continued publishing, and my average right now is about nine). In the kinds of academic fields that I am addressing in this book, I think that you will be surprised to find out how many of our colleagues, despite what seem to be reasonable and attainable numerical publishing goals, are not living the productive publishing lifestyle that they may envision for themselves. This formula gives you who wish to achieve such a lifestyle a reasonable set of goals to strive toward.

Never Say No

I have a number of professional colleagues who take a very different approach than I do to the issue of acceptance of writing and publishing opportunities. I have one friend who plots out all of his writing projects over the next several years, so that he will only take on a new project if he has an available slot between projects he has already signed up for and knows that he can accomplish. As a result, if he is asked about a new project and he does not believe that he can finish it within the time allocated, he will turn it down—sometimes he will try to make some adjustments if the new project is exceptionally important, but not usually. As a result, my friend has probably never missed a deadline or submitted a paper or manuscript late. I, on the other hand, have totally overcommitted myself—much to my friend's consternation and frustration—so that I usually hit my deadlines (eventually), but sometimes do not, and have a number of projects on which I am running way behind as a result. The difference, I believe, is that I have taken on far more projects—and as a result published far more—than my colleague has. My colleague takes on one project at a time and succeeds 100 percent of the time. By contrast, I take on ten projects and accomplish about seven of them. I only accomplish 70 percent of my projects or perhaps less, say 50 percent, but I accomplish much more than he does. I am sure that I frustrate far more editors along the way by missing a few more deadlines than he does, but I also make many more editors happier because of what I am able to accomplish for them. My colleague has published several very good books and a number of good articles. I have published over a dozen (I think) very good books and many more articles. One of the major reasons for this is that I say "yes" to virtually every project I am asked to contribute to. Now, I may take it a bit further than others do, but there are many good reasons I have for doing so—besides the obvious one that I continue to build up my publishing profile.

Some of the reasons that I accept so many projects are easy to understand. Yes, I am a bit obsessive-compulsive, and so I am obsessed with the challenge of writing and publishing one more thing, especially in a new area. Besides my psychological issues, I have other rationalizations as well—I mean, *reasons* as well. I am insatiably curious about intellectual things. I have ranged very broadly in my primary field of specialty, writing on many areas within it, because I have a short attention span for many intellectual topics. Once I have explored a topic and believe that I have a handle on it, I want to go on to the next thing or a related thing or at least something else. As a result, I have explored many if not most of the major areas of interest to me in my field, and many of the remote

nooks and crannies of it as well. I have also moved int
Actually my initial academic training was interdisciplin
different ways (switching subject areas, doing interdiscip
research), and I have continued along this line. I believe
plinary studies have much to offer the creative developme...
tual discipline, and I appreciate the intellectual stimulation and challenge
that interdisciplinary thinking offers. Publishing is in some ways harder
in interdisciplinary areas, because the work requires expertise in several
fields and can be marginalized as fitting comfortably in neither specific
camp. Nevertheless, interdisciplinary research has the decided advantage
of more easily being able to produce groundbreaking and unique work
because fewer people are exploring such intellectual interactions.

Another reason that I accept so many writing and research projects
is that I love knowledge, and I believe that you do not really know what
you know about a subject until you are forced to write on it. The writing
process itself is a form of intellectual exploration and delivery, which
encourages you as the writer to initiate, test, and develop your thoughts
in the course of writing itself. I have had many occasions when I believed
that I knew what I thought about a particular topic, until I began to write
on it. At that time, I realized a number of different things. Sometimes I
recognized that I did not know nearly as much as I thought I did, and
needed to do more serious research and exploration before I would be
able to make a significant contribution. Sometimes I realized that my
perspective or viewpoint was insufficient or skewed, and I was required
through what I learned while writing to change that perspective. Still
other times, I discovered in the course of writing that I was simply completely wrong on a topic and needed to rethink—which usually means
writing more—an entire topic. The writing itself is a part of the thinking
about and research on a topic.

A final reason for my enthusiastic involvement is that accepting such
writing and research opportunities opens up further occasions for writing
and publishing. This result may come about because I establish a new
area of interest and expertise, or it may come about because I am seen
by others as being willing to contribute to a project. For whatever reason,
I have found that my willingness to say "yes" to a variety of projects—
even in areas that I did not previously have expertise—has led to more
opportunities and recognition in areas that I would never have guessed I
would have been drawn to and in which I could make a contribution.

If you as a scholar are serious about developing a publishing lifestyle, you should consider supporting such a lifestyle in the actions that you take to accomplish and fulfill your writing goals. Writers have different patterns and habits of writing, and these must be adapted to the various requirements of life. The only general principle that I believe applies to all potential publishing scholars is that you must do more than simply talk about scholarship—you must actually do it. That means setting aside the kind of time that you need to be able to write. For some, this may mean short periods of time spread throughout the day and the week. For others, this may mean concentrated blocks of time, such as on a particular weekday or the weekend. For still others, it may be time at night when the house is quiet, or it may be in the morning before anyone else is awake. Some may need to go into the office or to another place, such as a library, in order to get work done, while others may work best at a home library with all of their familiar resources around them. One thing is certain—putting off writing until everything else is solved, done, and taken care of will mean that your writing and publishing will always be the last item on the agenda and rarely achieved, or only achieved for a short amount of time—enough to tantalize but ultimately only to frustrate. What I am trying to say is that developing a publishing profile requires a publishing lifestyle, and that lifestyle requires the discipline to set aside the kind of necessary time in the right environment to get the writing done. There is no point in accepting a number of good, worthwhile, and interesting research projects if there is no way in the world that you can get even one of them done, simply because the life patterns you maintain do not and will never allow for time to read, research, and write. Those important times should be built into your regular schedule as diligently as meal times.[4]

Paralysis of Overanalysis

A number of scholars whom I have met simply cannot force themselves to write for publication.[5] In fact, I have made a small uncontrolled study of some of these people. It is not that these scholars are not bright enough. They usually are. It is not that they are not well enough educated—again, they usually are, although I have to admit that some of them have gone through programs of study that have not done particularly well in preparing them for the life of scholarship by actually teaching them the trade of being a scholar, but instead have just had them take a lot of courses to accumulate knowledge (or usable notes). There seem to be at least two major reasons for not being able to overcome the hurdle of not publishing.

The first reason that I have uncovered is that the scholar is simply lazy. There are all sorts of factors that may contribute to this laziness, but, at the end of the day, such a scholar simply is not interested enough—because of holding a secure position or whatever—to get motivated enough to do anything of significance. There is not a whole lot that can be done about that, at least so far as I am concerned—except for your academic dean to start yearly or periodic evaluations and possibly encourage the person to find a new career for failing to meet contractual and/or reasonable expectations.

The second and far more serious reason is deep-seated insecurity. This insecurity comes from a number of different sources but often manifests itself in what I call the "paralysis of overanalysis." In other words, the scholar ends up finding all sorts of additional ways to analyze the data, results, writing, presentation, margins, spacing, watermark, color of the paper, envelope seal, address, and whatever else so as to avoid finishing the paper and sending it to the publisher. Sometimes the delay takes place at the level of failing to get research done—after all, there are always another couple of articles or a key book, or even a key book about to appear, that needs to be examined before you can hope to say anything important. Sometimes the delay takes place at the time of writing—the constraints of teaching provide for no writing time, or those necessary blocks of uninterrupted time cannot be found, or the desk needs clearing, or the dog needs walking, or the pencils need sharpening before you can think and get down to writing, to the point that serious writing cannot and does not take place. Sometimes it is because I think I need another test of the material—it is not enough that I as the author think that the work, now that it is finally done, is good enough, or that my in-house colleague in the field thinks that it is good enough. I need to get some outside scholar or, better, several scholars to read it before I send it off. The last reason—and I have seen this especially in a number of scholars who have particular ideological beliefs in relation to their subject—is that there are those scholars who are so afraid of being wrong, or, perhaps even more to the point, of not getting everything exactly right, that they are afraid to publish at all, and certainly afraid of venturing forth into new and untried areas.

There is a great scene in the movie *A Few Good Men* where the character played by Tom Cruise is talking with the character played by Demi Moore. They are both playing the parts of lawyers and talking about what happens in the courtroom. Moore thinks that court proceedings are about determining the truth. Cruise corrects her by telling her that it is not the truth but what he can prove in the courtroom that matters. I am not quite so cynical as to think that the truth does not matter or that there is simply a pragmatic rationale for research. However, for those who are hung up on the fact that they cannot publish until they are convinced that they have the absolute and complete truth, they perhaps need to see this movie. In one sense, for any given article, it is not about the truth, at least in a final and absolute way. Growth and development in any intellectual discipline involves a complex interplay of various pursued hypotheses, to see which ones get us closer to a truthful understanding of the subject. I think that it is unreasonable to believe that any given article or book will ever say all that needs to be said about any serious and important scholarly or intellectual area—unless it resorts to saying only the most banal trivialities. Instead, I think that we need to take the approach that all of our serious and well-intentioned efforts are steps along the way toward better understanding. There is a saying in the hard sciences that a negative result is also a result, because it indicates a direction not to follow. The humanities and social science disciplines are less attuned to accepting negative results as the positive results that they sometimes really are. Some explorations of a subject will prove to be more productive than others, but until these various ideas are laid out for scrutiny by a wider audience, they cannot enter into the discussion.

This is where the "paralysis of overanalysis" enters in. I have seen too many cases where scholars with something to say have been almost literally paralyzed because they believe that they need to scrutinize their work another few (hundred) times before it can be sent off to a publisher. I would encourage scholars with this problem to realize that, indeed, they may be wrong on occasion, and certainly may well be corrected, refined, or fine-tuned by others in the field, but that a serious effort needs to be published for it to be able to make any contribution to the field. Once this major hurdle and barrier has been overcome, I have seen that it can be a liberating experience for a scholar and help to set him or her on a path of productive scholarly activity.

The living of a publishing lifestyle does not occur by accident. I think that it can only occur by intention. In other words, those who want to live such a lifestyle need to set out to do so by design. This involves setting and achieving reasonable, and sometimes unreasonable, publishing goals. More than that, it involves developing a pace of publication that can be sustained over an entire career, from the enthusiasm of the early years all the way through to retirement. A career of lasting significance can only really be guaranteed by this kind of regular and continued publication. Along the way, there are certainly hurdles to be overcome, unfortunately many of them of our own self-making. If you can overcome these, you are on the path to living a productive and rewarding publishing lifestyle.

10

📖

LEARNING THE TRADE WITH OTHERS

The last topic that I wish to discuss is how you as a scholar aspiring to develop a writing lifestyle can build in the kinds of accountability structures to ensure both initial success and continuing productivity. As I have said repeatedly and tried to emphasize above, there is no substitute for simple and regular hard work. This hard work requires the kind of discipline that forces you to do the necessary reading and research, to carve out the mandatory time for writing, and to find the means to deliver the final product into the hands of the publishers. However, there are a number of other techniques that can often help this process go a little faster and more smoothly. I give five of them here that I have found useful through the years.

The five means to enhance a publishing lifestyle all involve working with others to build in accountability. These include (1) collaborative research, (2) involvement in the organization of your subject area, (3) the public instigation of projects, (4) research seminars, and (5) workshops.

Collaborative Research

I am a firm believer in the virtues of collaborative research, and I have therefore mentioned collaborative research a number of times in this work. I believe in collaborative research for a variety of reasons. Collaboration is an excellent way of working with and learning from others. Working with another scholar, or with other scholars, is often a very good means of benefiting from their learning and expertise, and of increasing your own expertise as you discuss various ideas. Collaborative research is also a way of generating new ideas for publication, because it has a natural way of expanding your boundaries to include new and different ideas that you would not have thought of on your own. Perhaps the most important feature of collaborative research, in light of developing a publishing lifestyle, is the accountability that it brings.

I have had numerous scholars promise to deliver to me a variety of chapters, articles, and even books. I do not believe that many of them were intentionally attempting to deceive me when they said they would do so. However, it is easy for a scholar to promise to deliver a particular work to an editor or someone coordinating a project. It is even easier to promise to yourself that you intend to sit down and do some reading and study on a particular topic, and to write up an article during the next available period of time, such as the winter break or summer holidays. Persistent editors can be dodged reasonably easily, until finally they will give up and reassign the work to someone else. Promises made to yourself, like promises made in foxholes, can be conveniently ignored, or certainly easily postponed into oblivion, once circumstances change. It is far more difficult, however, to ignore your own colleague down the hall once the two of you have agreed to work together on a given project.

I mentioned above my colleague who does brilliant PowerPoint presentations. We have worked together on a number of collaborative projects, and he is intellectually daring and insightful, and a lot of fun to work with. The one slight problem is that he tends on occasion to procrastinate, which can make collaboration a challenge at times. We were recent participants in a conference together, and we agreed to do two individual papers and then a joint paper. The night before the conference, my colleague—because he had the impending deadline of delivering a paper the next day—stayed up most of the night to put together a stunning PowerPoint presentation. This presentation went very well and was well received by the audience. For our joint presentation, he also prepared some PowerPoint slides. He unfortunately never converted his individual presentation into a finished paper, but he sent me a couple of paragraphs and footnotes and a couple of charts and the like for our joint paper, which means that I did most of the work to develop this into a final version of our joint paper. Most of my collaborations go more predictably than this one, including many of those that the two of us have worked on together, but even this one resulted in two papers for me, one more than I would have had if I had not undertaken the joint effort.

As a set of guidelines for developing collaborative accountability, I would suggest that you find other scholars whom you believe you can work with, and from whom you can gain encouragement and take direction without getting offended and pulling out of the project. Effective collaboration requires a willingness to give close and attentive scrutiny to the work of your collaborator, while also being willing to encourage and even goad the other into completing the project—all without the risk of losing the friendship or the collaborative relationship over it. This is not always easy to do, but I believe that the most effective collaborations grow out of this willingness to push the other person until the project is complete. I have been an active collaborator and have found it very beneficial. I have coauthored five books as collaborative efforts, most of my edited volumes are collaborative efforts (sometimes as a way of teaching a junior scholar the tricks of the process), and a surprisingly large number of journal articles and chapters have been written with others. Many of these have been opportunities to encourage younger scholars as they have been initiated into writing for publication. There is no formula for the division of responsibilities, as each collaborator brings something different to the task—that is what makes collaboration such a potentially enjoyable and rewarding exercise, as we work together to create something that goes beyond our individual efforts. Some of these collaborative projects have gone more smoothly than others, in that some have been unfairly one-sided arrangements, with one being forced to salvage the project or one needing to do more encouraging and cheerleading, but I have benefited from each one in a variety of ways. I have learned more about other subjects than I would have otherwise, to be sure, but I am also very convinced that I would not have accomplished nearly as much if I had not entered into such relationships. I believe that such collaborative efforts should be encouraged, and be more widely used than is now the case in such as areas as biblical studies, theology and religion, and the arts and humanities.

Subject-Area Organization

Another way of developing and keeping a publishing lifestyle on track is to be involved in the organizational dimensions of your academic discipline. Our professional and academic disciplines are, in many ways, at least as important to us as our academic institutional affiliations, because they provide a means of identity with those of common interests and perspective. Therefore, the maintenance and administration of such organizations is important to our own research development, and we can benefit from being involved in such activities.

Having said that, I think that I need to be careful how I talk about organizational administration, because I have seen some unhealthy developments in such areas, especially in institutional academic administration. There is an unfortunate tendency for a number of scholars whose careers stall somewhere around associate professor level—because they probably recognize that they may not readily achieve full professor and that they certainly will not receive the kind of academic fame and renown that they believe that they deserve—to slide over into academic administration. This is virtually always represented as a promotion, or an important career shift, or an answer to a call to an equally productive task. Let's not kid ourselves. The vast majority of such "scholars" (I use the term guardedly) are admitting that they cannot cut it as major players in the academic and intellectual world, and so they shift to an area where the working hours are saner, the intellectual pressures are lighter, and they can have power even if they do not perform well in terms of contribution to scholarship. This is the very thing that I am not talking about in this section, and that I would warn any aspiring academic to beware of.

The purpose for becoming involved in subject-area organization is not to hone your academic administrative skills, with the idea of moving to full-time administration, but to develop your organizational abilities so as to enhance the academic discipline in which you seek to make a more lasting contribution. By being willing to take on subject-area organizational tasks, such as being on a steering committee for a conference or subject group within a conference, or chairing sessions at meetings, or instigating constructive dialogue on topics among colleagues, you are able to effect a positive outcome on your discipline. Every subject needs good, competent practitioners within the field to be willing to spend time to enhance the quality of the discipline and how it functions. Involvement in subject-area organization provides such an opportunity to make a contribution in return for what your discipline has provided, such as opportunities for presenting papers, avenues for research and publication, and a willing audience for your publications.

Public Instigation of Projects

One of the major hurdles to overcome in pursuing a line of research and writing is that of actually beginning the project. It is one thing to think about the project, and perhaps even to read a couple of things to see if your initial ideas have merit. However, it is another thing to actually "take the plunge" and begin to focus on this particular area of research as something you intend to pursue for the next period of time. As a result, I think that it is important to establish a means of building in public accountability for the instigation of new projects.

These new projects may be collaborative—and a good number of them probably will be—or they may be individual. If they are individual, they should be heralded and publicly announced in such a way as to build in accountability from others—such as a spouse,[1] assistant, or even students—who will take an active interest in the work that you are doing. There are ways of ensuring that such encouragement and accountability are maintained. One may be simply to work out an agreed timeline with a spouse or colleague so that they can provide gentle reminders and prods to help you to continue your work. Another may be the instigation of a small in-house research group or series of talks that can be organized at your home institution. The first talk or talks can "announce" the intentions of your research project. You can then follow up these initial talks with periodic updates on progress as you discuss your developing findings. A research seminar paper is also a good means of making such a public statement. In a sense, even an individual project can become a collaborative project with built-in accountability as you share your work and progress with others who are interested.

If the project is collaborative from the outset, the fact of collaboration itself builds in accountability. I have found that collaborative projects, while good for almost any purpose, are especially good when there is an urgency to getting a publication out. I have found myself in situations where the publication of a recent book or the emergence of a "hot" topic demands a published response. In several of these cases, I have suggested to a colleague that if we were to work together on this project, we could capture the momentum of this particular topic, and perhaps make a constructive contribution to the debate. As a result, I have coauthored two popular-level books that have been timely responses to current issues. Working together as colleagues, we were able to complete a draft of each book in about six weeks, and then take a couple more to edit and submit to the publisher. As the issues were timely, the publishers responded promptly, and we were able to get the two books out. There is nothing like the tyranny of the urgent and the inquiries of a colleague to keep you working on a manuscript until it is done.

Research Seminars

The research seminar is a staple of the academic life of numerous institutions and can provide an important means of accountability in developing a publishing lifestyle. Research seminars can take a variety of forms. My first exposure to one was when I was a graduate student working on my Ph.D. My university had what was called a staff/student research seminar. This meant that on alternate weeks the academic staff would organize the list of speakers, and on the other weeks the research students were responsible. I ended up as the research student in charge of putting together the list of student contributors. This format provided occasion for the academic staff to present research in a challenging but supportive environment in which their colleagues and students heard the results of their work. The students had the opportunity to present work where they would be evaluated by both the faculty and their fellow students. On numerous occasions, we also had papers presented by visiting speakers from other institutions, at which time both faculty and students could evaluate the work of these outsiders. I think that the temperature in the room was definitely higher when the outsiders came onto our turf. Later, when I was at another institution, I instigated a research seminar for my faculty and students. One of the major differences was that, rather than simply having the faculty and students alternate presentations, we geared the presentations to coincide with where the students were in their programs. We also tried to ensure that the papers were prepared and distributed in advance, so that more time could be spent discussing the paper rather than hearing it read out. I have found both models of research seminars to be highly productive and valuable for both presenters and auditors.

What these research seminars had in common was that they provided opportunities for accountability in the presentation of research. It is one thing to talk about research you are contemplating or even involved in, but the entire level of involvement is significantly raised when you are asked to present your findings to a group of peers, whether these are faculty or students. Therefore, volunteering to do such papers is clearly of benefit as you are researching a particular topic. At this stage in my career, for the most part, I get other people to present the papers, although I try to be there as much as possible and to host the event if I am able to. It inevitably happens that, along the way, we will need a last-minute stand-in for a paper, or simply cannot find a person to give a paper on a given date, and so I will often be able to give a paper sometime during the year. These research seminars—besides having special value for developing scholars working on dissertations—give opportunities to hear what others are doing, to be stimulated in your own thinking by such work, and, perhaps most of all, to develop a new project that will lead to future publications. The research seminar makes a good place to give the first airing of such a project, and is especially conducive to working toward publication if it is prefaced by a statement to the effect that this is the first draft of an article on this topic, with an anticipated completion and publication date in, say, eight months.

Writing Workshops

The last proposal I am going to make may look, at first sight, a bit unusual and impractical, but I think that it has huge potential, and when the techniques that I am proposing have been used, they have often had tremendous results. I like to encourage the use of the writing workshop method as a way of encouraging the development of a publishing profile. I would be happy to come to your institution to lead such a workshop. Rather than pay me to do so, however, I am providing here a detailed treatment of what I would do in such a workshop, geared for self-implementation or implementation with a couple of encouraging and similarly interested colleagues.

The goal of such a writing workshop is to benefit from each other's encouragement, provide critical responses, and create mutual accountability. This is facilitated through the following steps: assessing your publishing profile, setting a realistic goal, developing a publication plan, doing the research and writing, engaging in collaborative editing, and submitting the manuscript.

Assessing Your Publishing Profile

The first stage is to do an individual assessment of where each person stands in the course of their development of a publishing profile and implementation of a publishing lifestyle. One of the best ways to do this is to examine your c.v. to see your record of publication. Oh, you don't have an up-to-date c.v. or résumé? This is the time to make sure you have one. Just in case you do not have an adequate c.v., I will provide some brief guidelines for developing one.

Let me make one clear statement at the beginning. The academic c.v. is about what you have accomplished, not about the dates that you did it. This is the major difference between an academic and a business or employment c.v. So, rather than running a list of dates down the left margin (continuous employment is a big deal in the business world), I think that an academic c.v. should list down the left margin the key items of accomplishment that are being chronicled, such as a publication or a degree earned, or the like. With that basic formatting issue out of the way, let me deal with the major parts of the c.v.

I prefer the style that simply places your name in large letters at the top of the first page—it is obviously a c.v., so you do not need to label it with the unnecessary word "Résumé" or whatever—and then, in a smaller font, your contact and other vital information, followed by educational details, with the highest degree listed first. Then I divide my c.v. into two major sections. The first section is concerned with employment information. This can be divided into as many sections as necessary but probably should begin with your academic positions, listing the position, place, date, and perhaps responsibilities, beginning with the current one. Other sections to add include such things as other academic positions (honorary and outside your primary institutions), academic administration, academic support including committees, training courses, grants and awards, consultancies and work for the wider profession, any editorial activities, and professional associations and affiliations. Some people also include a section that lists special interests and hobbies—one of these had better be writing! The entries in all of these sections should be listed in chronological order.

The next section is concerned with publications. There are two ways of organizing your list of publications. One is by type, and the other is by date (usually by year). I keep both lists but include the one by type in my c.v. I divide the publications into the following categories: authored books, edited books, journal articles, chapters in books, dictionary and encyclopedia articles, Web site articles and protocols, translations, book reviews, and conference papers and lectures. You can add a section for popular-level publications, if you wish. This list essentially reflects the order of decreasing importance, with the exception that edited books are placed after written books and before articles. I usually add an entry when I sign a contract to undertake the project, as in the case of a book, or when I have agreed to write an article or chapter—although there are many exceptions to this governed by my own need for record keeping. I then update the information as the manuscript proceeds through the publication process (e.g., from being "in process" to "in press" to full publication with details). At one of the universities where I used to teach, there was a yearly exercise of noting the publishing projects in which faculty members were involved—an excellent idea for developing mutual faculty accountability and informing of each other's interests. One of the categories that was used to describe publications was "early conceptual stage." This category may just as well have been called "vapor publication." I do not include such abstract and probably never-to-be-realized projects in my c.v. The other list of publications is by year, and here I enter every publication once it has appeared (but not before), so the list only includes those publications that have appeared, in their order of appearance. The advantage of the list by type is that you and others can see what kinds of publications you have done and are currently doing, according to category and hence relative value. The advantage of the list by year is that you can see the regularity of publication and quantity that goes with it according to a measurable unit of time.

Now that you have an accurate and up-to-date c.v.—I update mine every time something significant happens, such as I submit a finished paper to a publisher or editor, or have a book appear, etc.—you can assess your progress and pace of publication. One of the first tasks to be done is to perform the kind of mathematical calculation that I talk about in chapter 9. As a result, you should have an indication of the overall pace of your publication. However, the evaluation of overall performance could probably benefit from mining into the specifics. Here is where I think that discussion with a trusted colleague who might become a useful and encouraging ally and accountability person comes in handy. There is no point in fooling yourself into thinking that your publications are better than they are. Sometimes it is necessary to have a trusted colleague point out that it has been a few years since anything significant has been published, or that there seem to be no journal articles in the past number of years, or whatever. What is needed here is a hardheaded examination of what the state of play is.

Setting a Realistic Goal

The second stage in the process is to describe what you want the state of publication to be. Let's say that right now I am not even averaging a single publication a year. That means that I am not even publishing a single journal article or chapter every year, but perhaps one every two or three years. And there are no written books anywhere in sight. This does not look good. As a result, I decide—on the basis of having read this book and learned how straightforward publishing can be—that I want to increase my pace of publication to an average of one article per year from now on. That would be a reasonable goal. Perhaps later I may want to go back and raise my average for my entire career to one per year or even two per year—what I consider to be the desirable norm. This would mean that I would need to publish two, three, or four articles, and even some books, at regular intervals. But perhaps I am getting ahead of myself at this point.

Developing a Publication Plan

Once you have set a reasonable goal for your current circumstances, it is time to find a plan for accomplishment of that goal. Here is where your being connected to the rest of the scholarly world, having kept up your reading in the journals and relevant books and attending conferences, comes into play. I hope that somewhere along the way you have jotted down some notes on topics that could potentially be written up into papers. If you don't have a list of interesting ideas that you have not explored, then you need to get busy finding them. This book is full of suggestions on how to create and develop ideas like that. If you were really desperate, you might simply go to some of the latest journals in your field and see if there is any issue where you know that you have a defensible idea that is different from one recently published, and you can respond to it. This is just a start. I hope that this book has encouraged you to think more systematically about where such ideas may come from, and how to realize them.

In any case, you need to develop a specific game plan to become an active, publishing scholar. Through reading this book, perhaps you have noted some useful areas that you wish to pursue. Perhaps you have been reminded of a paper that you wrote in graduate school that received some encouragement but that you did not pursue at the time. Perhaps you realize that your dissertation—Has it been published? If not, why not?—still has some ideas that have not been fully explored elsewhere. The next stage is to take one or two of those ideas and determine to write a paper on this topic and complete it by a set date. I would even suggest a more specific plan—so many weeks or months for reading and research, so many weeks or months for writing, and so many weeks for producing the final product to submit. I would not suggest taking on more than is reasonable at this point—such as suggesting a multivolume set of lengthy monographs to make up for the fact that you have not published for the last ten years. Such unrealistic overambition is doomed to failure. Accountability or even collaboration can be very helpful at this stage, so that your best intentions and plans do not remain at the "early conceptual stage" and can actually become a "real publication," and not just a "vapor publication." I would put the plans in writing and give a copy of this timeline to your concerned colleague, or even to an interested friend or spouse who can help to keep you on track.

Doing the Research and Writing

The next stage is to research and write a complete draft of the manuscript, whether it is an article or a monograph, in the style of a reasonable publisher for that kind of piece. At this stage, if you have not been publishing regularly, an article-length manuscript is probably the best place to start, along with perhaps delivering a paper at a seminar or conference to test your work as it develops. If along the way there is some difficulty in structuring or writing the manuscript, I would suggest examining a number of recently published essays to see what they do that you can emulate so far as format and style are concerned.

Once the manuscript is in an acceptable draft, I would set it aside for a week and then return to it with ruthless intention. I would examine every sentence and every footnote to ensure that I am saying what I want to say and nothing more or less. I would check to be sure that I have the proper documentation presented in the right way. I would see if there are any sentences or paragraphs that are extraneous or don't make sense, and I would correct them. Let me repeat that I would encourage you to be ruthless and uncompromising at this stage in your self-critical analysis so that you have confidence that the work that you submit to a publisher has benefited from everything that you could do.

Engaging in Collaborative Editing

Once you have gone through and revised the article to your satisfaction, I would suggest then giving it to a colleague to have that colleague do the same thing. If I were meeting with you in a workshop, I would at this stage like to go through your work with careful scrutiny, questioning every place that does not make sense or that causes the slightest hesitation.

If you are doing this on your own, you will need to ensure that your colleague takes this exercise as seriously as you do. It is not always easy to find the right person to be involved in such an endeavor.[2] As I note above, your colleague is not helping you if he or she does not read with critical scrutiny, so it is best to find someone who will offer an honest opinion on the manuscript in all its dimensions. As educators, we may be willing to be quite critical of our students in their work, but we rarely are as critical of our colleagues' work. For a variety of what seem to be good reasons, we rarely want to be seen to be negative toward the work that they do. And I must admit that we are not very good at receiving such criticism. The tendency is to get defensive or argumentative when our peers make suggestions. I do the same thing—until I have had a chance to think about it for a while, and then I often realize that my colleague is right and that my argument does fall apart at a particular place.

I have often found that trust and collaborative responsibility can be built if two colleagues regularly work together on each other's writing. In other words, if you can find a colleague who also wants to build a publishing profile, the two of you can work together to scrutinize each other's work at regular intervals. This has several advantages. It makes the relationship reciprocal rather than one-sided. It develops the range of writing and publishing skills for both of you, as you are both engaged in writing and then scrutinizing each other's work. It builds trust and mutual respect, as each is subject to each other's comments. It may also lead to further intellectual discoveries and possible areas of further research and/or collaboration.

Submitting the Manuscript

At last, the manuscript is done. It has been read and scrutinized by you and by your colleague, and consequently revised until there do not appear to be any problems of fact or substance. You can breathe a sigh of relief, but the process is not done. The process is not done until the article is published. Now you must send the article to the publisher that you have identified as one most likely to respond positively. In the course of your research, you will have noted the possible places for such a publication and will have ensured that your manuscript falls within their parameters for subject, length, and documentation style. You must now send it to them in the format that they desire. Then, after anywhere from six to nine months, you wait for that e-mail or letter back that begins with those welcome words, "I am pleased to inform you . . ."—and you are one more step down the road to a productive publishing lifestyle.

Much arts, humanities, and related research and writing are done individualistically. The scholar is seen as lone researcher, poring over books in isolation and producing singularly authored works. There is nothing in and of itself wrong with such a model. However, I believe that there are ways in which scholars can helpfully aid each other in developing and then continuing a successful publishing lifestyle. These can involve a number of means by which scholars work together in aid of their discipline, rather than simply in competition with or even against each other—without in any way jeopardizing the individuality of their own research and publication. These collaborative efforts, which can take place at any number of levels of engagement, can result in works that have increased chances of publication and make significant contributions to their respective fields.

11

FINAL WORDS OF ENCOURAGEMENT

The world of academic publishing is often represented—by scholars, by publishers, and even by some of the guides to the field—as a complex and impenetrable world, full of all sorts of insuperable difficulties that only the fortunate or privileged can overcome. This is nonsense, as I hope that you have come to realize from reading this book. However, there are some scholars who have a vested interest in maintaining this veneer of complexity. Sometimes they do so in order to make themselves seem more important or to make it appear that they have accomplished more than they really have. Sometimes they do so in order to protect a particular position of importance that they think they are entitled to within the guild. I trust that I have shed light on the entire publishing process, so that it is no longer seen to be any sort of mystery but simply a business with its various protocols. I hope further that I have shown that the possibilities of scholars working together in a common endeavor actually provide much more opportunity for shared success than does resistance to providing access to avenues of publication.

I have long been intrigued as to why it is that publishing companies often wish to perpetuate a similar sense of distance and remoteness. I think that some of this is attributable to the fact that, for the most part, publishing companies want to be seen as representing noble values such as knowledge, truth, and the like, when in reality they are governed by, even slaves to, basic economic principles, and these ultimately guide their decision-making processes. Publishers know deep down that these are not necessarily the best of motives for making decisions on scholarship, and even on people's professional lives. Publishers and scholars must recognize that they need each other—publishers need scholars to provide the material that serious publishers require to stay in business, and scholars need publishers to provide legitimate avenues for dissemination of knowledge. Forming productive and beneficial relationships between scholars and publishers is in the best interests of each, as they support each other's work. One of my aims is that this book will provide a means for scholars to be on a more even and informed footing for dealing with publishers, and that publishers will respond positively by helping to create opportunities for scholars to produce further publishable research.

As for those books that do not provide as much information as possible on the inner workings of academic publishing, I simply have no explanation to offer. The only thing I can think is that those writing such works—many of which have some useful information, but do not penetrate to the heart of the business—perhaps have not had the opportunities to learn what I have regarding academic publishing and hence are not able to open up the kinds of possibilities that I hope that I have outlined in this book.

It would be a mistake, however, to think that it is other scholars, publishing companies, or even books on how to publish that hold the primary responsibility for the development of your publishing career. At the beginning and end of the day, that primary responsibility rests with you and you alone.

There are almost countless legitimate opportunities in the world of academic publishing for you to publish and disseminate the products of your research and writing. These opportunities include a number of different vehicles for productive scholarly research, such as monographs and books, edited collections of essays, refereed and other types of journal articles, chapters in collected volumes, encyclopedia and dictionary articles, and even book reviews. Each of these potential types of publication provides an opportunity for a different type of contribution. What they have in common is that there is a particular way in which such successful research is to be presented in written form. One of the major ways to begin to see the possibilities that each has is to always consider writing with publication in mind, and then gear your lectures, teaching, and conference papers toward such publications. Publishers themselves also have a variety of standards that they expect to be maintained in the work that they accept for publication. Your learning of these expectations and standards will enable you to craft your work so that its presentation is suitable for publication by the publishers of your choice. Even if you receive rejection letters in the course of your attempts to publish—and it is almost inevitable that you will—you should learn from these rejections. If you continue to refine your craft, by selecting suitable publishers for your work, presenting your manuscripts in an appropriate format, and benefiting from the comments and criticism of trusted colleagues, I believe that you will almost assuredly be greeted with inevitable letters of acceptance. Once these letters of acceptance begin to arrive, you can continue to develop, and even increase, the pace and types of publications that you produce. The pace and types of publications can be developed through a variety of means in which you generate new ideas for publication, develop new areas of research, and engage in productive collaboration with others. Rather than making scholarship an individual sport, the more you can share in it with others, the more such collaboration can increase your possibilities of significant and interesting publication. The result is to develop and live a publishing lifestyle that makes a lasting and enduring contribution to the scholarship in your academic field.

It is no mystery how successful scholarship is done. It is not done with smoke and mirrors or with incantations and spells. It certainly is not the domain of only the few or lucky or elite. Like any field of endeavor, however, there are tried and true ways in which such scholarship is done in order to be most successful. In my experience, these means are often not explicitly discussed but are either assumed or left for potential authors to discover accidentally or only through lengthy experience. The goal of this book has been to provide a handy and explicit road map to the ways in which, at least for me, successful scholarship develops from inception to manuscript, and from manuscript to final publication, both to take away the unnecessary mystery and to help to provide a clear guide for potential success. After all, as I trust this book makes clear, successful academic scholarship does not occur by accident, but it only occurs as the direct result of focused and intentional action by you as a publishing scholar.

Notes

Introduction

1   This is not all that I do, I must admit. I have coauthored several popular-level books and edited a number of others. We even sold the movie rights to one of the popular-level books, and an independent film producer has used that book as the basis of a made-for-television documentary. I have also written regularly for the popular press, including authoring a regular column for a biweekly newspaper. These, how-ever, are not the focus of my major research and thinking, and not the purpose for my writing this book.

2   In fitting academic form, I should probably offer a footnote about other works that treat this subject of academic publishing (I do not claim to have read, and certainly do not claim to have agreed with, all of them in whole or in part). Some of these include Joseph M. Moxley, *Publish, Don't Perish: The Scholar's Guide to Academic Writing and Publishing* (Westport, Conn.: Praeger, 1992); Robin M. Derricourt, *An Author's Guide to Scholarly Publishing* (Princeton: Princeton University Press, 1996); William P. Germano, *Getting it Published: A Guide for Scholars and Anyone Else Serious about Serious Books* (Chicago: University of Chicago Press, 2001); Beth Luey, *Handbook for Academic Authors*, 4th ed. (New York: Cambridge University Press, 2002); and G. Patrick O'Neill and Robin P. Norris, *Scholarly Writing Worthy of Print* (London, Ont.: Althouse, 2006). See also William P. Germano, "How to Be an Author," *Chronicle of Higher Education*, January 14, 2008.

3   This experience was invaluable in giving me an inside view of the academic publishing business. See also Rachel Toor, "Understanding Academe, Authors, and Editors," *Chronicle of Higher Education*, May 4, 2007.

4   See Stanley E. Porter, "Is a Doctorate All That Is Necessary?" *Faculty Dialogue* 20 (1993–1994): 125–29.

Chapter 1

1   In his *Animal Farm*, George Orwell depicts the pigs as believing that, though all animals are equal, they are "more equal" than the other animals.

2   Incidentally, in case you were wondering, my Ph.D. is from the only department (at that time) to get the top rating for my primary subject three RAEs in a row,

including for the period of rating during which I received my degree. I myself was rated at international level for my personal research when I was heading my own department in the UK—I told you there were bragging rights attached.

3   The problem of the limited market and relatively high cost of traditional book production—this process requires that the publisher invest in all of the costs of producing the book, including editing, printing, and binding, before procuring any sales—is addressed in various ways in different countries. Some use a subvention system, while others simply charge outrageous amounts for their books. In Canada, where I currently live, the number of academic publishers is very small, and the potential market, especially for books with Canadian content, is relatively small as well. As a result, there has grown up a subvention system that relies upon securing government-funded (or research council-funded) subvention grants. This simply results in overly inflated subvention demands, and the even more outrageous expectation that taxpayers unknowingly pay for books that they will never see or use and which probably have little to no direct or indirect impact on their lives.

4   The thesis statement that guides all of the writing will often need to be even more specific in its formulation, including the enumeration of key lines of support or argumentation.

5   For those not up on their footnoting types, citation footnotes consist of reference to a source that in some way supports a point being made in the text, while content footnotes argue for points that are not essential to the main argument of the text but offer tangential though necessary support. In some disciplines, one sometimes finds the perspective that content footnotes either should be included in the text or dispensed with altogether because they are not essential to the argument. Footnote 4, in the introduction above, is a citation footnote, while this one is a content footnote. I obviously think that there is a role for content footnotes. (My editor obviously agrees.) I will comment more on footnotes and their styles below.

6   In some disciplines, such as linguistics, it is considered appropriate to cite simply the author and date in the social-scientific citation, without page number, unless a direct quotation is used. I find this frustrating, as it makes it very difficult to trace the specific origins of an idea.

7   I am not technically dealing with a monograph here but with a type of book. See below for further discussion of other types of books.

8   I am not a lawyer, so I am not attempting to give legal advice on such matters as copyright. I am, however, writing on the basis of my experience both as an author and as an editor of journals and monograph series.

9   As noted above, this is not legal advice, and if you are tempted to do this and want to know how much change constitutes creating a new work, you will wish to consult a lawyer. However, publishers can usually be convinced to allow you to reuse your own material, and so this should not often arise as an issue.

10   Okay, you got me. I claim expertise in the area of academic publishing, and this is my first (and probably my only, but who knows) book on how to publish. I guess I could say that all of my other publications support my claim in this book. Then again, this is not normally considered an academic discipline.

11   As I look back on it, I think now that this is one of the reasons that the book did not sell particularly well or fast and was taken out of print by the publisher after the first print run—it was simply too much book for what it was designed to be. I am proud of this book and think that it is still the best in the field, as I think it provided things that most other textbooks in the area do not.

12   What it takes to become a recognized literary agent is not defined. There are no degrees or examinations required—only stationery and perhaps a mail drop.

13   See Dedi Felman, "What Are Book Editors Looking for?" *Chronicle of Higher Education*, July 21, 2006.

14   See Rachel Toor, "No Bad Authors," *Chronicle of Higher Education*, June 29, 2007.

15   See Clement Vincent, "Don't Judge a Book by Its Editor," *Chronicle of Higher Education*, October 22, 2007.

16   See Thomas Kuhn, *The Structure of Scientific Revolutions*, 2nd ed. (Chicago: University of Chicago Press, 1970), 144.

17   See Thomas H. Benton, "Reference Works and Academic Celebrity," *Chronicle of Higher Education*, December 9, 2005.

18   There are increasing efforts worldwide to rate and rank journals. A number of countries and regions have tried to establish and maintain such lists. The criteria for such lists are often unclear, and there are many disputes over the resulting rankings. Nevertheless, such metrics appear to be growing in use and significance, and so you should begin to pay attention to such rankings for placement of your publications.

Chapter 2

1   That my reaction was not unique is validated in Jeffrey J. Williams, "Confessions of a Journal Editor," *Chronicle of Higher Education*, September 28, 2007.

2   See Rachel Toor, "My Left Tackle," *Chronicle of Higher Education*, July 27, 2007.

3   Some of the works that I have looked at that may have value include Chris M. Anson, Robert A. Schwegler, and Marcia F. Muth, *The Longman Writer's Bible: The Complete Guide to Writing, Research, and Grammar* (New York: Pearson Longman, 2006); Toni Boyle and K. D. Sullivan, *The Gremlins of Grammar* (New York: McGraw-Hill, 2006); Glen R. Downey, *The Fifty Fatal Flaws of Essay Writing* (London, Ont.: Althouse, 2002); Alastair Fowler, *How to Write* (Oxford: Oxford University Press, 2006); Noah Lukeman, *A Dash of Style: The Art and Mastery of Punctuation* (New York: Norton, 2006); Martin Manser and Stephen Curtis, *The Penguin Writer's Manual* (London: Penguin, 2002); Bonnie Trenga, *The Curious Case of the Misplaced Modifier: How to Solve the Mysteries of Weak Writing* (Cincinnati: Writer's Digest Books, 2006); and William Zinsser, *On Writing Well*, 7th ed. (New York: HarperCollins, 2006).

4   I have even noticed that such a structure is taught in some books on academic writing for publication. See Sheridan Baker, *The Practical Stylist*, 4th ed. (New York: Crowell, 1977), 18–25.

5   I realize that actual thesis statements will probably be much more complicated in their structure. My point here is to illustrate the difference between a subject or topic and a thesis—the thesis must say something insightful and useful about the subject that you wish to argue and develop.

6   See Porter G. Perrin, *The Writer's Guide*, 4th ed. (1950; revised by Karl W. Dykema and Wilma R. Ebbitt; New York: Scott, Foresman, 1965), 65–67.

7   See Anthony Weston, *A Rulebook for Arguments*, 2nd ed. (Indianapolis: Hackett, 1992).

8   On signposts, my thanks to Nigel Gotteri, extraordinary linguist and friend. On being concerned for the reader, see Rachel Toor, "The Care and Feeding of the Reader," *Chronicle of Higher Education*, September 14, 2007.

Chapter 3

1   Another may be that reading books written on converting dissertations into books is often nearly as intimidating as writing the dissertation itself. Two recent efforts to help ease the pain are William Germano, *From Dissertation to Book* (Chicago: University of Chicago Press, 2005); and Beth Luey, ed., *Revising Your Dissertation: Advice from Leading Editors,* updated ed. (Berkeley: University of California Press, 2008). Unfortunately, there are some misleading or unfortunate statements in some of these books. For example, in "Frequently Asked Questions," Luey's book states that "[i]t is more difficult and time-consuming to print footnotes rather than endnotes" (p. 242). With computer typesetting—including authorial submission of the electronic files—there is no tangible difference that I know of. Also, Luey's book provides a five-year plan for converting the dissertation into a book and beginning the next project (pp. 247–52)—the author who follows this slow course my well be putting his or her career at a serious disadvantage!

Chapter 5

1   See Lynn Worsham, "What Editors Want," *Chronicle of Higher Education*, September 8, 2008.
2   Joking aside, I have had the opportunity to work with a number of excellent copy editors, whose level of professional and academic competence and attention to detail are phenomenal. I have encountered them through some of the most unexpected circumstances and appreciate them greatly. I trust those I am thinking of will recognize themselves in the description.
3   For quick reference, kerning is when the typesetter uses variable spacing between letters usually to adjust lines of type, leading is the space between lines (once determined by placing strips of lead between them), a hard space links two words as inseparable, loose lines have too much space between words and often require hyphenation in the lines above to correct the problem, hyphenation varies by publisher but should not be overused in consecutive lines, en dashes are longer than a hyphen and em dashes are longer still, and widows and orphans are short single lines separated from the rest of their paragraphs and left at the top or bottom of a page.

Chapter 6

1   See Rachel Toor, "Reject!" *Chronicle of Higher Education*, October 5, 2007.
2   This is an area where there has been quite significant shift in recent times. It used to be that scholarly writing had to be in the third person, with impersonal references to the author as "this writer" or "the author" or the like. Then the first person plural became the person of choice, so that "we" were always holding to various opinions. I always had trouble with determining who "we" were, especially if I did not follow or agree with the argument of the author—"you" and who else, if it is not me? I also find that it sounds quite artificial. I think that first person singular is the best person for writing scholarly prose. "I" then take responsibility for what I am thinking and writing, and you may or may not follow, but at least I am not trying to linguistically ambush you by use of inclusive language. Some editors and some publications have not yet come around to the brilliance of this stance, however, and so, if they demand first person plural or third person impersonal, "this author" suggests that "we" write that way to keep them happy and get published.

Chapter 7

1   This term is still used, even though we are long past the days when someone actually sets up type with letters in long lines to form the template—the original mean-
ing of the term "typesetting."

2   This stage certainly does *not* include sending an entirely new manuscript back to
the publisher, with your additions and changes included in it. This may seem self-
evident to most, but I have been surprised to see the number of authors who think
that proof stage is an excellent opportunity to begin again with their manuscript.

3   Seeking a lawyer's advice may well be the best step to take with regard to these
clauses.

4   These are only rough lengths of time, based on my experience. There are many
variables to consider.

5   I know of several publishers that claim to have lost submitted manuscripts. I
strongly recommend that you check back with a publisher if you have not heard
anything from them in a year. If they have lost the manuscript (and admit it!), I
would strongly consider trying a different publisher.

Chapter 8

1   As a side note, I usually do not distribute my papers at conferences or provide anything more than a one-page outline. I also usually do not send copies to those who
inquire, until after I have had the paper accepted for publication. I want to be the
one to control the presentation of my ideas in print.

2   Just as a matter of insight, I virtually always end up rejecting papers and proposals
by the (often self-appointed) guru figures when they appear to be simply trading on
popularity rather than on substance, and seem to be more interested in high-profile
performances than genuine scholarly discussions. I find it intriguing to note that a
number of nonliterary scholars have taken to writing poetry, music, and even nov-
els. These works are about as good as you would expect them to be coming from
scholars in completely different, nonartistic fields.

Chapter 9

1   There are various ways of estimating and calculating scholarly productivity. See
Robert Wuthnow, *The Struggle for America's Soul: Evangelicals, Liberals, and
Secularism* (Grand Rapids: Eerdmans, 1989), 164, for discussion of Lotka's law.

2   I do not recommend this, as I noted above, but use this here for the calculation. I
believe that the dissertation should be published within the first two years or so
after completion, and then the next book five years after that. A scholar then might
be able to publish eight monographs in a full career. (Incidentally, who says you
have to stop publishing at sixty-five years old?)

3   For another take on this, see David Perlmutter, "Your 50-Year Career Plan," *Chronicle of Higher Education*, April 27, 2007.

4   If you do not eat meals regularly, you should perhaps be concerned about this too.
As this is not a self-help guide, and I do not have any expertise in nutrition, I will
leave that topic to others—and get myself a snack.

5   See Thomas Schmidt, "How Not to Write a Second Book," *Chronicle of Higher
Education*, March 30, 2007.

Chapter 10

1   Having a spouse supportive of your research and writing can make a huge difference to a publishing career. I know of one person who told me that his spouse
would not allow him to talk about his scholarship in the house. Those of you who
are still single and contemplating a publishing career may well wish to take this
into account when considering marriage partners.

2   See Rachel Toor, "Editing Friends," *Chronicle of Higher Education*, January 6,
2009.

Index